Praise for
The Wisdom of Titans and Bill Ferguson

"In *The Wisdom of Titans*, Bill Ferguson brings together a who's who of entrepreneurs who candidly share lessons learned on their journeys. The book contains important commonalities—passion, focus on the bottom line, growing market share, developing a team—as well as "secret sauce" ingredients unique to each individual. This is a must-read for anyone who is or wants to be a successful entrepreneur."

—Jeffrey Fox, Fox & Company,
author of the bestselling *The Transformative CEO*

"Being your own boss is the great American dream, but only 1% of entrepreneurs are truly successful. Ferguson, chairman and CEO of Ferguson Partners, interviewed some of the world's best-known entrepreneurs in order to instruct a wide audience: entrepreneurs whose businesses have stalled; corporate leaders who want to take a more entrepreneurial approach; budding entrepreneurs; and M.B.A. students....[the] interviewees instruct the reader to have fun at work, be a student of the business, make a mark outside the mainstream, grow the bottom line, mentor others, create value out of a vision, take risks, measure progress, maintain integrity, and leave a legacy...the overall message is strong."

—*Publishers Weekly*

"What does it take to be a successful entrepreneur? In *The Wisdom of Titans*, Bill Ferguson goes to the source to answer that question—the top executives and highly successful business builders across industries from hospitality to health care. Their 'success secrets' encompass solid business practices as well as those unique traits and qualities that make a difference between good and great. This book is a game-changer for anyone interested in the entrepreneurial journey."

—Thomas Priselac, president and CEO,
Cedars-Sinai Health System

"Driving growth, managing risks, navigating uncertainties, and growing profitability—admittedly, it's a tall order, but in reality these are merely table stakes for entrepreneurs today. In *The Wisdom of Titans*, Bill Ferguson engages in insightful and compelling one-on-one conversations with notable entrepreneurs whose experiences reflect the best practices needed for entrepreneurial success today. An engaging and very worthwhile read."

—Ian MacMillan, Ambani professor of Innovation and Entrepreneurship; director, Sol C. Snider Entrepreneurial Research Center, Wharton School of Business

"Successful entrepreneurs today are those who not only have the next best idea, but who also have the vision, drive, and discipline to execute that plan into reality—while developing a team that will take a startup to the next level and beyond. Those who do it exceptionally well are a rare breed, indeed. With more humility than pride, they muster the courage to take on challenges to build what becomes both scalable and sustainable. In short, they become titans. In *The Wisdom of Titans*, Bill Ferguson gathers a who's who of business builders who have built their success over the years and now graciously share what they've learned and experienced along the way."

—Kevin Brown, president and CEO, Lettuce Entertain You Enterprises, Inc.

"*The Wisdom of Titans* provides an invaluable inside look at what it takes to build a sustainable and scalable business, drawing from those who have done it. Ferguson's book is a real gift for anyone interested in understanding what it takes to become a truly successful entrepreneur."

—Harry M. Jansen Kraemer, Jr., author of the bestselling *From Values to Action;* former chairman and CEO, Baxter International; clinical professor of Management and Strategy, Northwestern University's Kellogg School of Management

"No matter what industry or niche you're in, you will find true wisdom from these 'titans'—those who have reached the pinnacle of achievement in their respective fields. As their stories and examples show, it's not enough to have a great idea or an executable plan. Entrepreneurs must possess key qualities and attributes, such as passion, drive, vision, integrity, discipline, and the willingness to be both a student of the business and a coach and mentor of others. For anyone who is interested in the entrepreneurial path, this is the essential roadmap."

—Denny Shelton, chairman of the board, LHP Hospital Group Inc.; former chairman & CEO, Triad Hospitals, Inc.

THE WISDOM
OF TITANS

THE WISDOM
OF TITANS

SECRETS OF SUCCESS
FROM ENTREPRENEURS
WHO ROSE TO THE TOP

WILLIAM J. FERGUSON

bibliomotion
books + media

First published by Bibliomotion, Inc.
33 Manchester Road
Brookline, MA 02446
Tel: 617-934-2427
www.bibliomotion.com

Printed in the United States of America

Library of Congress Cataloging-in-Publication Data

Ferguson, William J.
    The wisdom of titans : secrets of success from entrepreneurs who rose to the top / William J. Ferguson.
        pages cm
    Includes bibliographical references and index.
ISBN 978-1-937134-58-7 (hardcover : alk. paper) — ISBN 978-1-937134-59-4 (ebook) — ISBN 978-1-937134-60-0 (enhanced ebook)
    1. Entrepreneurship. 2. Success in business. 3. Leadership.
4. Business enterprises—Management. 5. New business enterprises—Management. I. Title.
    HB615.F474 2013
    658.4'09—dc23
                    2012050831

This book is dedicated to all entrepreneurs who pursued their passion to become titans.

CONTENTS

FOREWORD   xi

ACKNOWLEDGMENTS   xv

INTRODUCTION   Tapping the Wisdom   1

CHAPTER ONE   Have Fun at Work   5
J.W. "Bill" Marriott Jr., Executive Chairman,
Marriott International, Inc.

CHAPTER TWO   Be a Student of the Business   23
William "Bill" Sanders, Founder, LaSalle Partners Ltd.
(now Jones Lang LaSalle) and Security Capital Group
Incorporated, Co-Founder, Verde Realty, and Co-Founder
and Chairman, Strategic Growth Bank Incorporated

CHAPTER THREE   Make Your Mark Outside
the Mainstream   39
Stuart Miller, CEO, Lennar Corporation

CHAPTER FOUR   Grow the Bottom Line—Period   55
Noel Watson, Former CEO and Current Chairman
of the Board, Jacobs Engineering Group Inc.

CHAPTER FIVE   Coach, Mentor, and Teach Others   69
Julia Stewart, Chairman and CEO, DineEquity, Inc.

CONTENTS

CHAPTER SIX Create Value out of a Vision 83
Robert L. Johnson, Founder, Former Chairman, and CEO,
Black Entertainment Television

CHAPTER SEVEN Be True to Yourself 97
Sam Zell, Chairman, Equity Group Investments

CHAPTER EIGHT Take a Risk to Do Things Differently 111
Richard "Rick" Federico, Chairman and CEO,
P.F. Chang's China Bistro, Inc.

CHAPTER NINE Measure Your Progress at Every Step 125
Paul J. Diaz, CEO, Kindred Healthcare, Inc.

CHAPTER TEN Be Mindful of the Shadow You Cast 139
John Robbins, Founder, American Residential Mortgage
Corporation and Past President, Mortgage Bankers Association

CHAPTER ELEVEN Make the 2 Percent Difference 155
William A. "Bill" Jensen, CEO, Intrawest

EPILOGUE The Differentiators 169

NOTES 175

INDEX 177

FOREWORD

The key ingredients to building a great company come down to what I call the three P's: passion, persistence, and patience. Passion fuels the fire and sustains the drive to do the difficult, but exciting work involved with launching (or relaunching) a business. Passion reminds the entrepreneur and the entrepreneurial-minded leader alike of why they do what they do. It is motivation and direction combined. Persistence is the strength to stay the course to enact change, which can be challenging on both the personal and organizational levels. When the path to meaningful change meets resistance, persistence shows the way around, over, or through the obstacles. Finally, patience reminds us that anything worth doing well, takes time. Patience honors the process that allows the essential lessons (including from mistakes made along the way) to be discovered and absorbed.

Since becoming President and CEO of Hilton Worldwide in 2007, I have used the 3 P's every day to lead the transformation of a nearly 95-year-old global organization, with more than 300,000 team members at our corporate offices and owned, managed and franchised properties across 10 brands and in nearly 100 countries. It started in my first 100 days as CEO, when I literally traveled the globe, talking to people in the company about what they saw as the greatest needs to transform our organization. To a person, I heard a consistent message about the desire for more cohesion within our company, which had grown largely through mergers and acquisitions over the years. We needed to bridge those gaps so that being part of Hilton Worldwide, and the culture it represented, brought us together on common ground. This is the charge I brought back to the senior leadership team, as we gave our all to motivating, aligning, communicating with, and leading our team in a new and better direction.

We reached back to the legacy of our founder, Conrad Hilton, a great entrepreneur who started this company in 1919. In 1943, Hilton became the first coast-to-coast hotel operation in the U.S. Also in the 1940s, Mr. Hilton created for our company a slogan that contained a powerful vision: "to fill the earth with the light and warmth of hospitality." This message connects all of us, no matter where we work or what job we perform, from accountants behind the scenes to the housekeeping staff on the front lines of serving our guests. It remains as true today as it did 70-plus years ago.

That is what entrepreneurs do. They create a vision that spans functions, operations, locations, and even decades, providing a "North Star" to which the organization can continually orient itself. When things get off track, as they undoubtedly will from time to time, a strong vision will point the way back to the core values that separate an organization from its competitors.

In these pages, readers will find excellent advice, examples, and lessons learned from the most notable of entrepreneurs—the titans, as author Bill Ferguson calls them—who have left their mark in a variety of industries, all of which are people-intensive service businesses. Ferguson has amassed a who's who of entrepreneurial leaders who share their experiences in creating and growing businesses, while capitalizing on opportunities, weathering economic storms, and facing global competition. Their success has come from technical and tactical knowledge and expertise, but, more important, from their personalities and their characters—their entrepreneurial DNA.

By sharing their stories, these titans demonstrate that entrepreneurs, by their very natures, are generators of plans and ideas. They see what others do not: the untapped market, the unmet consumer demand, the potential in a niche that remains off the radar of their competitors. With creativity and commitment—and the 3 P's of passion, persistence, and patience—they find a way to bring a concept to life.

But no leader can go it alone. As Ferguson so wisely points out, a true differentiator between a person who starts a business and a successful entrepreneur who sustains an organization is the ability to develop a team. Those who make it to the next level are those who have the honesty and self-knowledge to admit where they are weak and purposefully surround themselves with people who are strong in those areas. The entrepreneur who becomes a titan looks beyond himself to others who must execute the strategy every day.

This is the age of empowerment. Entrepreneurs who embrace this truth will gain an edge over those who see business building as an exercise in self-determination or, worse yet, ego. Big or small, local or global, a company is known by the people who touch consumers each day. An organization can circle the globe, but it's the people on the ground who make the measurable difference.

FOREWORD

Whether you have founded a business (or intend to) or have been entrusted with taking an existing enterprise to the next level, you will face considerable challenges. Simply stated, entrepreneurship is not easy. It will take everything you have to give, and then some. But the difference you can make in the lives of others, especially your customers and colleagues who work with you and for you, is the best of rewards.

Good luck to you in every endeavor. May your path to success be engaging and rewarding, with valuable lessons to learn and to share along the way.

Christopher J. Nassetta,
President & CEO, Hilton Worldwide

ACKNOWLEDGMENTS

There are several people to acknowledge for their contribution to this book. Top of the list, of course, are the "titans" who graciously shared their insights and experiences: Bill Marriott, Bill Sanders, Stuart Miller, Noel Watson, Julia Stewart, Robert Johnson, Sam Zell, Rick Federico, Paul Diaz, John Robbins, and Bill Jensen. Without them, this book would not have been possible.

I'd also like to thank my publishers, Erika Heilman and Jill Friedlander, and the entire team at Bibliomotion for their enthusiasm, guidance, and commitment to this book. I am truly grateful for this opportunity to spread the word about what entrepreneurship and good leadership is all about. I also thank my agent, Doris Michaels, of DSM Literary Agency, for her vision and support for this book.

In this and all my undertakings, I want to thank my wife, Andrea Redmond Ferguson, who allowed me to make time to write, edit, and critique this manuscript. Not only is she a great partner, but she (as an author herself) truly appreciates the time requirements necessary for such a massive undertaking.

I want to thank Kim Chantelois who patiently scheduled these multiple interviews and worked through the transcription process, and Julia Gier, for all her efforts to market and

ACKNOWLEDGMENTS

promote this book and our other editorial endeavors. And thanks to Tricia Crisafulli, our manuscript consultant.

Finally, I want to acknowledge all the entrepreneurs and other business leaders with whom I've had the pleasure to work and interact over the years. Individually and collectively, you are an inspiration.

Introduction

Tapping the Wisdom

What does it take to become a successful entrepreneur? Is it a specific talent or an inborn quality? What roles do early influences, opportunities and experiences, and even luck play?

These were the questions I had in mind when I began researching and writing *The Wisdom of Titans*. Entrepreneurs are a unique breed in the business world, particularly those who, against the odds (the success rate is about 20 percent) launch their own businesses. Those who truly make it, who reach a pinnacle of success, are rare indeed. Thus, to define what it takes to be a successful entrepreneur, I went to the top, to some of the best-known business builders in their fields. The result was a pantheon of talent—the "titans," as I call them—representing the 1 percent of entrepreneurs who really make it, those whose companies expand nationally and globally, whose employees typically number in the thousands and even tens of thousands.

At the same time, I wanted lessons meaningful to many, those in small firms as well as large ones. My intention is to appeal to a varied audience: entrepreneurs at every stage, including those who are experiencing slowing growth or whose businesses have stalled; current and aspiring corporate leaders who want to adopt a more entrepreneurial approach to generate and sustain growth; people who are considering starting their own businesses; and MBA students and others who are interested in studying the habits of successful leaders. With this broad audience in mind, I set out to find the heart and soul of entrepreneurship, the "success secrets" that make all the difference and can be best learned by doing. For that, I had to tap into the "wisdom of the titans."

In these pages, you will hear from: Bill Marriott, executive chairman, Marriott International; Bill Sanders, founder, LaSalle Partners and Security Capital Group, and co-founder Verde Realty and Strategic Growth Bank; Stuart Miller, CEO, Lennar Corp.; Noel Watson, chairman, Jacobs Engineering; Julia Stewart, chairman and CEO, DineEquity, Inc.; Robert Johnson, founder, Black Entertainment Television; Sam Zell, chairman, Equity Group Investments; Rick Federico, chairman and CEO, P.F. Chang's China Bistro; Paul J. Diaz, CEO, Kindred Healthcare, Inc.; John Robbins, founder, American Residential Mortgage Corporation; and Bill Jensen, CEO, Intrawest.

With more than thirty years' experience recruiting and advising CEOs, senior executives, and board members, I've had the privilege of meeting and getting to know people with extraordinary talent and success in business building, including entrepreneurs and company founders, as well as people who've turned around businesses or taken them to the next level. I've witnessed firsthand the difference that culture, customer-oriented employees, the right incentive structures, and well-integrated staff and operations across global geographies can make. And, I've also seen the impact of character and discipline among a distinct and rare breed of leader: those who have transformed a concept and a vision into the reality of a large and vibrant business (which for some means a global, publicly traded empire).

After interviewing the eleven titans for this book, and based upon my knowledge of and interaction with many others, I found a blueprint—a recipe of behaviors and attitudes, if you will—that truly makes the difference. This blueprint includes: "have fun at work," because it's the passion for the business that will keep you going; "be a student of the business," learning from within your own industry as well as across the breadth of the business landscape; "don't make your mark in the mainstream," instead seek out the underserved niches; "coach, teach, and mentor others," paying close attention to the development of your team; "be mindful of the shadow you cast," because your integrity is visible to others at all times; "make the '2 percent difference,'" with a commitment to do the extra that makes an impact on customer satisfaction; and many more.

The leaders in this book come from a variety of industries, from entertainment to health care and from real estate and hospitality to engineering. The common thread among them is the importance of service. Brands, technology, and processes aside, what makes these companies successful are the people who have customer contact, whether the customer is a patron at a dining table or a patient in a clinic. For these titans and their businesses, their intellectual capital is riding up and down elevators and walking the halls. And it starts with the titans themselves. Long before these individuals were big names in business, they were hardworking people with an idea, a concept, or a plan; they found opportunities and seized them with passion, driving themselves to learn all they could and make a difference.

Talking with these gifted and distinguished individuals was a privilege not only because of their accomplishments, but also because of their willingness to share their lessons along the way. The bigger the titan, the more he or she could chuckle over the early mistakes, while pointing out the invaluable lessons gained in the process. In every instance, these titans gave credit to role models, mentors, partners, and, above all, their teams. Their humanness and humility were disarming and refreshing, which perhaps serves as the biggest success secret of all: your business is not just about you. Although you need a healthy ego and a good deal of confidence to launch a business and make your mark in a highly competitive arena, you can't do this for yourself alone. Building a business is ultimately about others: your customers, your vendors and partners, and above all your team. These are the people who will voyage with you along the entrepreneurial path. You will learn with them and from them.

I wish you much success on your entrepreneurial path, wherever it takes you, whether you are starting your own company or helping to grow an existing enterprise. Within the world of business, this is one of the most satisfying experiences, to witness the growth of an idea into a concept, a concept into a plan, a plan into a strategy, and a strategy into a business.

Chapter One

Have Fun at Work

> ...if you can't have fun doing what you're doing, you'd better find something that you enjoy doing because you won't be successful unless you do.
>
> —J.W. "Bill" Marriott Jr., Executive Chairman,
> Marriott International, Inc.

Becoming an entrepreneur takes energy and drive. Achieving success takes an unrelenting commitment to turning an idea into a plan, a plan into a start-up venture, and a venture into a sustainable business that generates a return and creates opportunities. For the entrepreneur—whether the founder of a business or the leader who takes an organization to the next level—a tremendous effort is required. Simply stated, the business is all-consuming.

The payoff, therefore, must be a level of intrinsic satisfaction that outweighs any extrinsic reward. Even when an entrepreneur creates wealth, the result often pales by comparison to the sheer time, money, and hard work invested. The only real motivation, therefore, is passion. Among entrepreneurs, from small business owners to titans with business empires, what they do for a living is the reason they get up in the morning. Even during challenging periods when work can hardly be called fun, the engagement they have in the business provides tremendous satisfaction and motivation. For any entrepreneur launching a new business or trying to expand and grow an existing operation, the secret to success is to be emotionally and intellectually engaged. Passion and engagement are paramount.

From working in his father's restaurants to running a premier global hospitality company with brands such as Marriott, The Ritz-Carlton, Residence Inn, Courtyard, Fairfield Inn & Suites, and SpringHill Suites, among others, J.W. "Bill" Marriott Jr. has shown a true passion for the business. Today he is executive chairman and the recently retired CEO of Marriott International, the hotel management and franchising company, which has more than thirty-seven hundred properties in seventy-four countries and territories worldwide.

With more than fifty years of leadership at the company he founded, Marriott clearly qualifies as a business builder. While working alongside his father, company founder J. Willard Marriott, he was instrumental in expanding the business from restaurants and food service into hotels; later he spun the operating company off from the property-owning company, which became a New York Stock Exchange–traded real estate investment trust (REIT), Host Hotels and Resorts, chaired by his brother, Richard Marriott. As a result, the Marriott International portfolio shifted from hotel ownership to managing and franchising properties.

During our conversation, Marriott credited much of what the organization has become to the legacy of his father. In fact, throughout our conversation, Marriott referred numerous times to his father and the lessons learned from the man who had a strong work ethic and demanded excellence of others, especially his sons, to the point of perfectionism. Equally telling, however, was the point of departure between Marriott and his father on the topic of work and passion. For the elder Marriott, the emphasis was always on the tasks and responsibilities that needed to be accomplished each day with great attention to detail. However, the younger Marriott—for whom excellence in delivery and execution was no less important—added another element that has been essential to his leadership and which stands as a lesson for all business builders: do what you love, and love what you do. As Marriott's experience shows, without passion, there is no long-term success.

Love What You Do

Bill Marriott grew up in the family business, which in the early days consisted of a chain of restaurants called Hot Shoppes. During high school and college, Marriott worked in a variety of positions, from washing dishes to cooking hamburgers to working with the chef to prepare food for lunch and dinner. When Marriott went to college at the University of Utah in Salt Lake, his father had just opened a restaurant there, which gave him an in-depth learning experience in addition to his formal studies. "I learned the restaurant business, and I really loved it," Marriott recalled. "I thought it was great fun. I loved the action, I loved the excitement, and I loved the fact that it was very fast paced."

Marriott's passion for the business was clearly a major motivator in the formative years of his career, as he tried to meet his father's expectations while also distinguishing himself by his accomplishments. Although he worked hard, going to work was fun—a description his father never would have used. "There was always an emphasis on the work ethic—never an emphasis that work should be fun," Marriott recalled of his father's example and teaching. "His [the elder Marriott's] answer was, 'That's why they call it work.'"

The younger Marriott, however, had a different attitude, one that became part of his hallmark as a business builder. "My answer was if you can't have fun doing what you're doing, you'd better find something that you enjoy doing because you won't be successful unless you do."

A common trait among entrepreneurs is a real love of the business and genuine appreciation for those with whom they've shared the experience. Many, like Marriott, have grown up in a family business, which they later took over and expanded or transitioned into new directions. Some have started businesses from scratch, and others have been recruited to lead businesses that needed a turnaround or revitalization to take them to the next level. Regardless of the kind of entrepreneur you are or strive to become, no amount of business acumen, practical experience, or knowledge can make up for a lack of deep passion and unwavering commitment. If these emotional components are lacking, attaining success will be difficult, if not impossible, and any achievement will be lacking in satisfaction.

As Marriott recalled his early days in the restaurant business, his fondness for the experience was palpable. During college, Marriott was Navy ROTC, and later joined the Navy and trained in the Navy Supply Corps School. He became a ship's store officer onboard an aircraft carrier and was eventually put in charge of the ward room, which took care of food service for the officers. After his discharge from the Navy in 1956, his father assigned him to the company's restaurant test kitchen for six months. Then, in January 1957, came a turning point for the company and for Marriott. His father opened the company's first hotel: the Marriott Twin Bridges Hotel in Arlington, Virginia. At the age of twenty-four, Marriott approached his father with a bold proposition: "Why don't you let me go run that hotel?" When his father replied, "You don't know anything about the hotel business," the younger Marriott rose to the challenge. "I know," he told his father, "but neither does anybody else around here. We're all restaurant people."

With that, Marriott took a supervisor job at the first hotel, working closely with the general manager, an experience that allowed him to learn the business from the ground up. As the company built one hotel after another, Marriott expanded his knowledge and his business acumen. The driving influence in his life, however, remained his father, by word and example.

Fatherly Influence

"He was a perfectionist," Marriott said of his father, who had spent his early life on a "little dirt patch of a farm west of Ida, Utah." J. Willard Marriott never went east of the Wasatch Mountains until his trip as a Mormon missionary at the age of nineteen, which took him to New England and New York. When the elder Marriott returned to Utah during the Depression, his family was broke, having lost the money they borrowed to raise sheep. At age twenty-one, J. Willard Marriott had no money, no education (his father frequently pulled him out of school to herd sheep), and no opportunity. What the elder Marriott did have, however, was incredible resolve and a drive for self-improvement. For example, he carried a notebook in which he would write down every word he heard but did not understand. Later, he would look it up in a dictionary and memorize the meaning. As a result, he had a fabulous vocabulary.

Accepted into Weber Academy, a two-year community college in Ogden, Utah, the elder Marriott attracted the attention of a teacher who recognized his potential and encouraged him. Later, he attended the University of Utah, where he met his future wife. After they married, the two moved east and opened a root beer stand in Washington DC in May 1927. When the weather began to get cold, they expanded the menu to include hot dogs, hamburgers, chili, and tamales, and the Hot Shoppe concept was launched.

Next, in 1937, the elder Marriott launched the first airline food service business in the basement of one of the restaurant kitchens across from what was then Hoover Field, where the Pentagon is now located. He got the idea of preparing food for airlines after noticing that customers frequently came into the Hot Shoppe near Hoover Field to purchase boxed lunches. When he asked them why, he was told they were flying to Boston, New York, or Miami, but Eastern Airlines did not serve any food on board. This gave the elder Marriott the idea to fly to Miami to meet with Eddie Rickenbacker, the former World War I flying ace who had purchased the airline from General Motors. He convinced Rickenbacker that serving boxed lunches on board would be a competitive advantage. Marriott's airline food service business eventually had kitchens in Newark, Chicago, Washington, and Miami to service Eastern, and then other airlines as well. "We were the largest airline caterer in the world when we sold the business in 1989," Marriott recalled. "One of the keys to building a successful business is always to look for opportunities. My father was tremendously aggressive about finding opportunities."

As the company continued to grow, it took over food service for the Treasury Department, expanding the commissary menu with pastries, ice cream, and meals to take home—whatever the customer wanted. "If somebody came in and wanted apple pie a la mode with brown gravy on it, they'd get it," Marriott remarked with a smile.

For entrepreneurs in any industry, paying attention to the details and making sure that customers get exactly what they want are crucial to success. Customer loyalty builds brand equity, whether the product is a sandwich, a hotel room, or the latest technology gadget. In the competitive hospitality industry, Marriott has been able to standardize the guest experience in a very positive way that distinguishes its brands. "In our business, in the service business…anticipating the needs of the customer and the guests [is key]. If you're checking in and it's late at night, and you're tired and you want this feather pillow, we will get you a feather pillow," Marriott remarked.

Reflecting on his father's leadership, Marriott also described innovations over the years that extended beyond the hotel properties themselves. He recalled how his father "really loved and respected the hourly worker," which prompted him in the 1930s to establish the first medical program in Washington DC for hourly employees. In the 1940s, he put a doctor on the payroll to take care of employees, many of whom came from poor backgrounds and did not have access to health care. In addition, the elder Marriott invested in training, which he considered not only essential for excellent customer service but also for staff retention and motivation. This is a lesson for other entrepreneurs: if there is a problem with morale, it is the company's problem, not the employees'. One highly effective way to address it, as Marriott found, is with training and by laying out a path by which people can grow, develop, and advance their careers. "I've told our people, if we have a problem with morale someplace and people are not happy on the job, go in and train them. Train, train, train," he said.

Only by being given authority and the ability to make mistakes and learn from them can people stretch and grow. A leader, after all, is not in the business of telling people what to do, but rather in giving them opportunities to demonstrate what they can do. "That's the way people develop themselves," Marriott added. "Then they're excited about a company where they can measure their contributions and say, 'I did this and I did this, and I was instrumental in doing this.'"

Developing employees and making them feel valued is a centerpiece of the company culture, which Marriott credits to his father. "He was really, really good at taking care of his people. He developed the culture we talk about today, which is to take care of your people and they will take care of the customer, and then the customer will come back. He respected all people and they responded in kind, because there weren't very many companies back then in the '30s and '40s that really reached out and cared for people."

At the same time, his father demanded excellence of all his employees and held the operations to a high standard. Marriott recalled how, back in the 1930s, his father visited every Hot Shoppe restaurant each week: looking over the food, making sure the parking lot was hosed down at night (the restaurants were drive-ins, so the grounds could get dirty with spilled food), and ensuring that the kitchens were spotless. "I used to go on Friday inspections with him when I was in high school...I'd go along just to learn. He'd inspect four or five Hot Shoppes from soup to nuts, with a white glove inspection."

Calling his father a "tremendous student of the business," Marriott also described how he spent a month in California every winter, visiting any new restaurant he could find, particularly drive-ins that were similar to Hot Shoppes. "He'd make notes and bring back recipes and menus. He'd bring back wrappers and napkins—anything he could, to think about how it would fit into his business," Marriott described. "I think that's what gave him the courage to have the instincts that he could move ahead and do some other things (such as the airline catering business)."

From that experience, Marriott learned a valuable lesson, which he regards as key advice for any business builder: "Find out what's going on. Understand the needs of the customer and take care of the needs of the customer. Some people start making a little bit of money, and then they sit in a nice fancy office with their feet on their desk. They don't put their feet on the ground and get out, beating the bushes."

From its roots in restaurants, the business expanded into hotels, when the elder Marriott built the world's largest motor hotel, with 365 rooms, in 1957. At the time, President Eisenhower had launched an interstate highway program, which sent Americans traveling by car. The Holiday Inn hotel chain responded, and soon signage for these hotels appeared along the highways. Marriott's response was also to get into the business, but with bigger hotels. The first properties were located in Virginia, New Jersey, Philadelphia, Dallas, and Atlanta.

Bill Marriott continued to innovate in the hotel business, launching Marriott Rewards, a loyalty program that allowed customers to accrue points for discounts and free lodging. At the time, the program was unique, allowing Marriott International to retain its customers and attract others from competitors. Such innovation came from being a great listener and observer, and from knowing what customers want and being cognizant of the competition, which made Marriott an intense student of the business. Like his father, Marriott gets out into the field, visiting several hundred hotels a year. He has a reputation for arriving unannounced, walking the floors, and talking to customers and staff.

In the 1970s, Marriott wanted to expand more aggressively in the hotel business, but his father did not want to load up the balance sheet with debt. As his father told him, "I love owning hotels, but I don't want the debt." Marriott recalled, "I said, 'You can't own them without the debt.' Then he said, 'I won't own them, and I won't build any more.'"

With excess debt capacity, the company branched out instead into theme parks in Santa Clara, California, and Gurnee, Illinois. On the restaurant side, it bought Bob's Big Boy and Farrell's Ice Cream Parlors, and added Host Airport operations. Although the elder Marriott was reticent to expand the hotel side of the business aggressively, the company eventually added properties and brands. Marriott recalled that someone in the company suggested that they build smaller hotels, like La Quinta was doing at the time; "I said, 'Well, if they can make money in hundred-room hotels, then so can we."

Interestingly, Marriott International did not just rely on ideas from those inside the company, but retained a research firm to ascertain what the customer wanted. No surprise, the response was a "great room at a cheap price." This simple concept, which was self-evident, points to the humility of being a business builder; sometimes you need someone else to tell you the obvious. Marriott knew the only way to achieve both objectives of value and price was to reduce certain services and amenities (no doorman, no bellman, no big meeting rooms or ballrooms). "We kept it simple, really simple," he explained.

Between 1983 and 1989, the company opened 180 properties under its Courtyard by Marriott brand, which caters to business travelers. Also in the 1980s, the company bought Residence Inn, an extended-stay brand, and created Fairfield Inn & Suites, followed by SpringHill Suites. It then bought The Ritz-Carlton, a premier hotel chain, and Renaissance.

Throughout the expansion—and at one point because of it—the company faced challenges. But as Marriott had learned from his father, his most influential mentor, there was always a solution to be found if he was willing to work for it.

CEO PERFORMANCE OBJECTIVES

Whether they're start-ups or mature firms, companies need leaders who are capable of taking the company in the right direction—especially during challenging times or even crises. There are several factors to be considered, which will be weighted differently according to the type of company, its stage of development, and its strategic and operating requirements. Examples of key CEO traits and abilities include:

■ Vision: Has the CEO articulated a clear vision that makes good business sense? Does the vision provide a solid foundation for building the business? Do operating plans reflect this vision?

(continued)

- Leadership: What is the CEO's leadership style? Does it fit the company's needs? Has the CEO developed strong management that functions as a team? Does the CEO replace weak managers in a timely fashion?
- Integrity: Does the CEO set the tone for the company by exemplifying consistent values of high ethical awareness, honesty, fairness, and courage?
- Achievement of corporate performance objectives: How well does the CEO meet financial and operating performance goals, both short and long term? What are the CEO's abilities to achieve strategic targets? Are shareholder value goals and competitive performance factors taken into account? Are quantitative measures of performance set and tracked?
- Succession planning: Has the CEO proposed a succession plan that makes sense? Are the candidates viable and acceptable to the board?
- Shareholder relations: Does the CEO encourage open lines of communication between the company and shareholders? Is the CEO responsive to legitimate shareholder concerns?
- Stakeholder relations: Does the CEO build effective relations with employees, customers, and the community?

"Figure It Out"

One of the most formative lessons in business building can be summed up in three words: figure it out. As entrepreneurs discover, problem solving is a regular endeavor if not a daily routine. Often, one problem solved leads to another challenge later on; such is the nature of the beast as a company grows and expands, particularly in a new market or an underserved niche.

Marriott learned this lesson from his father, who would tell him, "Here's the problem; come up with a solution." The first solution he devised, however, would often be rejected, which sent him back to the drawing board for an alternative approach, until the problem was solved. "So you'd go back and work on it again. That's the way it was for nearly forty years of working for him."

When Marriott told the story, there was far more admiration than complaint in his voice. As he saw it, his father's objective was always to build up his reasoning, thinking, and ability to get things done. However, there were times when it was difficult, if not downright impossible, for Marriott to meet the standards of his perfectionist father. "I worked for him for thirty-eight years, and he was never satisfied," Marriott commented.

A few times in his younger days, his father's approach almost became too much for Marriott, and he thought about quitting the company. His mother was an important encourager, telling him to "hang in there," as he recalled. Yet a few times Marriott tried to submit his resignation to his father, telling him he couldn't handle the pressure any longer. "You can't quit," his father always told him. "Your name's over the door, same as my name. You're part of this family. You're not quitting. You're not going anywhere."

After trying to quit in frustration once or twice, Marriott decided not to go back to get the same answer the third or fourth time. And so he stuck with it, and as a result became as exemplary a business builder as his father had been. Therein lies an important lesson for any entrepreneur: the way forward will be strewn with difficulties, many of them seemingly insurmountable, but perseverance is the only way to advance. Virtually every entrepreneur at one time or another is on the brink, and must draw upon resilience and tenacity to keep moving forward. In so doing, business builders also develop emotional and cognitive "muscles" for times when much bigger challenges arise.

The working and mentoring relationship between the elder and younger Marriott was colored by the fact that they were father and son, a complex tie that brings with it the mixed desires to please and to push away, to rebel and to conform. For Marriott and his father, however, the dynamic appears to have been one of setting a high standard and then stretching limits to attain it. Yet, there are also times when the experienced elder must take on the role of the mentor, to guide as well as to encourage.

Marriott recalled an incident when he was company president, a title he had been given in 1964 at the age of thirty-two. Although he could not recall the specifics of the problem, he remembered it being "complex and difficult," and as a result he was "really discouraged" because he could not find a workable solution. He turned to his father for advice and, after a fifteen-minute conversation, it became clear to the elder Marriott that his son was stumped and could not move forward. Marriott's father shifted to a mentoring role as he walked his son step by step through the solution. "He knew the answers to everything he'd ever asked me to do. But he wasn't about to let me know that he knew the answers until he saw me hit rock bottom and he knew I had to be picked up. Then, he picked me up," Marriott recalled.

Throughout their careers, business builders will be faced with complex and difficult challenges, times when it is not only helpful but essential to turn to a trusted advisor. In addition, as

Marriott experienced later in his career, having a strong and talented team made up of people with complementary skills is an essential part of the solution. Indeed, great leaders are those who are comfortable cataloging their own strengths and weaknesses, and gathering a team with complementary talents and abilities. The best also have the confidence to hire people who are smarter than they are, and who will push the leader and not just be a yes person. The highly competent business builder welcomes the team member who asks, "Why can't we think about doing things another way?" Fortunately, Marriott had such a team, which helped him weather a very difficult storm of high debt and economic downturn.

The company's growth plan saw the Marriott chain expand through the 1980s with the opening of major properties, including the San Francisco Marriott Marquis, the New York Marriott Marquis at Times Square in New York City, and the Boston Marriott Copley Place. By the late 1980s, the company had $3 billion-worth of hotels on its balance sheet. Under Bill Marriott's leadership, the company began to shift away from owning all the hotel properties to selling them to limited partnerships and other investors. The Japanese were eager buyers of properties in the United States, largely because land and building prices in Tokyo had skyrocketed to levels that made them unaffordable. Then the Gulf War hit in 1991, followed by an oil crisis and a recession. Real estate investment dried up, and foreign money went home.

The company faced a severe cash flow problem. Hotel companies were going bankrupt, and the scuttlebutt on the street was that Marriott Corporation could be next. The answer to its cash crunch was found in its airport terminal food service operations, a solution that Marriott credited to the company's chief financial officer, Bill Shaw. At each of the airport terminal food service operations, there were as many as thirty cashiers, each with a "bank" of $500 that was locked up at night and picked up the next morning. Shaw's solution was to reduce the number of banks to four, which in total helped to increase cash flow across the system by several million dollars. With the increased cash flow, the company was able to pay down a portion of its debt, including $1.5 billion in revolving loans.

The company took other steps, including shutting down Marriott's construction department, which had been building Courtyard properties through the 1980s and into the 1990s. The only way to get financially healthy again was to look aggressively for savings in its operations in order to keep running and preserve as many jobs as possible. The strategy worked, and the company came out of the recession of the early 1990s in better financial shape than it had been in before. Marriott International also learned a valuable lesson that triggered a permanent change in its business strategy when it spun off from what is now known as Host Hotels and Resorts. Marriott International got out of the real estate business and concentrated instead on managing and franchising properties. "Let other people have the benefit of ownership and we'll take the management side," Marriott said. "That way you don't have a heavy balance sheet, and you can grow much faster."

The company's ultimate decision about what would carry it into the future most profitably and securely harkened back to the attitude of the elder Marriott, who had been very uncomfortable with taking on debt and committing capital to hotel building. As it turned out, the elder Marriott's instincts were correct and that strategy proved to be right. Looking back, Marriott credited his father's thinking, which turned out to be enlightened and ahead of its time, with establishing an operating model that the rest of the hospitality industry has largely followed.

Regardless of the industry, one also has to be cognizant of leverage, as we learned in the financial crisis of 2008, when high levels of debt became toxic to companies. All companies need capital to invest; some investments, like real estate, which involves hard assets, will require more capital than others, such as operating companies, which spend on people, systems, marketing, and so forth. Regardless of how it is deployed, capital is finite. Using leverage to make up the shortfall is dangerous. Business builders need to be smart about the businesses they are in, how much capital they consume, and how much leverage they are utilizing.

From a father to his two sons in the business, the Marriott family leadership has spanned more than eight decades, just as operations have expanded from the first root beer stand in the late 1920s to one of the largest and most successful global hospitality companies today. As the business changed over the years, new approaches and different solutions were deployed. Yet some elements of leadership have remained the same, becoming the foundational blocks of business building.

TIPS FROM THE TITANS

- ☞ Embrace passion and engagement as critical ingredients to having fun at work. Loving what you do encourages you to be a student of the business and immerse yourself in learning everything you can to improve the operation.
- ☞ Develop highly competent and empowered teams. Every person, regardless of title or position, must be valued.

- ☛ Emphasize training to improve skills, promote retention, and attract employees who want to be part of a successful and growing organization.
- ☛ Recognize that growth is not just a way to make more money; it serves a higher purpose to provide opportunities for people to grow—which enhances retention and facilitates recruitment.
- ☛ Empower teams to act independently, giving people challenges and allowing them to make decisions. Don't micromanage. Give people room to move and grow.

Chapter Two

Be a Student of the Business

> *Niches that are underserved, but where dramatic change is anticipated, can become fertile ground to capitalize on opportunities that others do not yet see. Reaping those opportunities requires a viable and relevant strategy, as well as a team that is aligned with the capabilities and cultural orientation of the organization and its goals.*
>
> —William "Bill" Sanders, Founder, LaSalle Partners Ltd. (now Jones Lang LaSalle) and Security Capital Group Incorporated, Co-Founder, Verde Realty, Co-Founder and Chairman, Strategic Growth Bank Incorporated

When launching a business, your ideas are not the only ones that count. Successful entrepreneurs—even those who are convinced that they do, indeed, have the proverbial better mousetrap—look far and wide for input that informs and influences their business strategies. Within their own industries, they search for underserved niches and evidence of emerging consumer needs that will translate into future demand and could transform the business. In other words, they seek opportunities before they become obvious to others. The real differentiator, though, is looking beyond one's own territory. The high achievers, who have known success in more than one venture, make it a point to study other businesses and industries, identifying best practices that they can apply.

The objective is to become a student of the business: always reading, listening, and learning. High-achieving entrepreneurs purposefully and continuously study such things as the habits of successful leaders and the business strategies that made the difference between good and great. One notable example is William "Bill" Sanders, who, over the course of his forty-plus-year career in real estate, has created huge opportunities in niches that others failed to see. In the process, Sanders, who is known to be a leading innovator in real estate management, founded two flagship firms: LaSalle Partners (now part of Jones Lang LaSalle, a global real estate services firm) and Security Capital Group, which spawned several real estate investment trusts (REITs) and was later purchased by GE Capital. As Sanders advises, "Ideally, you want to look for that one [niche] that everybody else is not pursuing, and where there is going to be radical change. That will develop an enterprise that can achieve an economic return that is very attractive."

For more than four decades, Sanders has been a transformative influence in real estate. Historically, the industry has had a transactional focus (and, in many cases, still does) as brokerage firms emphasize buying and selling properties. Sanders, on the other hand, took a different path by identifying the needs of corporate clients with regard to managing their real estate portfolios. Specifically, Sanders recognized that corporate clients would ultimately evaluate the real estate assets on their balance sheets in the context of their corporate strategies before making property decisions about buying, developing, leasing, or managing. This belief led him to take a nontraditional pathway into the corporate client. Rather than trying to sell services to the head of corporate real estate, he went directly to the key decision maker: the CFO. Not only did this executive hold the corporate purse strings, he also tended to be more strategic and took a dispassionate view of real estate. In contrast, corporate real estate executives were threatened by the prospect of a third party usurping their power and influence. The takeaway lesson for entrepreneurs in any business is not only to identify the potential need, but also the decision maker and how to access him.

Entrepreneurship in His Genes

Entrepreneurs are a different breed. They view the world as imbued with opportunity; that is, the world holds opportunity for those willing to look for and capitalize on it. Like other titans profiled in this book, Sanders had a nose for business from a young age; his first business was selling soda and crackers to golfers through a gap in the fence on the thirteenth hole of the local country club. "It was a high-profit business because my parents bought the crackers and the Cokes and I didn't have any overhead. It was a 100 percent margin deal," he laughs.

His business ventures became more serious by the time he was a senior at El Paso High School, in Texas. Hybrid Bermuda grass was becoming popular in the Southwest, and Sanders's father, who loved landscaping, suggested that he get into the business. Young Sanders started a hybrid Bermuda grass farm and made about $10,000, which was a lot of money in 1959.

Then, having learned the grassroots of the business, as it were, he was ready to strike out on his next adventure: Cornell University. His parents strongly encouraged the move to expand his horizons beyond El Paso, and told Sanders that they would help him pay for college if he attended a university more than a thousand miles from home.

His public high school education was no match for the private prep school backgrounds of many of his peers. In fact, during the first quarter of his junior year at Cornell, he and two classmates were voted most likely *not* to succeed. Fortunately, Sanders proved them wrong (as did the other two classmates, who ended up running global companies, one in the United States and one in Europe). Sanders held his own and graduated from Cornell's College of Agriculture and Life Sciences in 1964. (Today, he serves on the advisory board of Cornell's Baker Program in Real Estate and received Cornell's Entrepreneur of the Year Award in 1999.)

Looking back on his college career, Sanders concluded that 20 percent of his personal development came from what he learned in the classroom and 80 percent came from his peer group. His experience early on is similar to that of many entrepreneurs: often, they have the odds stacked against them and, as a result, have to work harder than anyone else—an experience that helps them to remain grounded, never forgetting where they came from and their early struggles.

After college, Sanders went to Honduras to work in what he called a Peace Corps–type program. Upon returning to El Paso, he founded International Development Corp; in 1970, he moved the company's headquarters to Chicago and renamed it LaSalle Partners. The company quickly set its sights on a niche market: corporate real estate services, at the time virtually unknown in the business. Such services would distinguish LaSalle among its more transaction-oriented competitors, giving the firm what he called "a highly relevant strategy."

Have a Highly Relevant Strategy

There are two basic kinds of strategies. The first is a plan based on what an entrepreneur believes will work, which may or may not prove to be accurate and successful in the long run. The second is a highly relevant strategy, which doesn't just happen. To be relevant is to be acutely focused on the customer, whether a corporate client or a retail consumer. As Sanders observes, "There are a lot of businesses that are highly successful for six years and then they burn out. This is because their strategies do not have strategic relevance." Strategic relevance equates directly to growth opportunities and longevity.

As LaSalle Partners began offering real estate services, Sanders recognized the disconnect within many large corporations between their corporate strategies and the deployment of capital required to buy, build, and manage real properties. For example, a large company in those days would spend $50 million or $75 million to build a headquarters, without much reflection on whether that was the best use of capital given its corporate strategy. The alternative was to hire a firm such as LaSalle Partners to develop the headquarters with the corporate client as the anchor tenant. Once the building was fully leased, LaSalle Partners would sell it to another entity, such as a pension fund, REIT, or investment fund. In the end, the corporate client had a new headquarters and was able to recoup its capital and probably make a profit. Even more important, the Fortune 500 had capital on its balance sheets to reinvest in its core business.

Because of this strategy, LaSalle was able to offer strategic value-added services, which the transaction-oriented traditional brokerages were not able to do. In time, LaSalle Partners became the second-largest property manager in the United States. That success was directly attributable to having a highly relevant strategy valued by customers.

Having the Right Culture for the Job

In successful organizations, culture supports and is aligned with strategy. A key component of culture is compensation. If all parts are not in sync, the business suffers. To learn more about highly effective corporate cultures, Sanders spent ten hours a week or more reading about the most successful businesses in the country, including blue-chip leaders like IBM. He learned that firms with customer-centric strategies hired people with the same focus and compensated them accordingly. He also found examples on Wall Street, which in those days focused more on advisory-oriented investment bankers earning healthy six-figure incomes and servicing the needs of clients, instead of proprietary traders who today make seven figures. That prompted Sanders to take a closer look at his own staff and how compensation matched up with the culture and mission of the firm.

By 1973, LaSalle Partners had one hundred employees, most of whom were paid straight commission, which was the norm in real estate. That pay structure, however, put the emphasis on transactions, which was not in keeping with LaSalle Partners' customer-centric culture. After Sanders retained consulting firm McKinsey & Company to undertake a compensation study, the decision was made to convert the compensation structure to salary with a bonus for reaching certain targets, and stock options granted based on performance. This new compensation system paid people based on the profits of the business rather than as a percentage of income, as the commission system represents. As the new system was implemented over the next two years, 80 percent of the LaSalle Partners staff left—the "cowboys" who were more interested in earning a commission than providing excellent service to large corporate customers.

Although Sanders admits that he did not think he would lose most of his revenue producers—his plan had been to change their thinking to accept a salary and a bonus—in retrospect, he considers it "the best thing that ever happened to me in business." The dramatic turnover allowed him to hire people who were closely aligned with the LaSalle Partners culture and the firm's objectives. In hiring replacements, he looked outside the real estate industry, recruiting professionals such as IBM marketing representatives. Sanders did not care that they didn't know real estate; what mattered most was having the right cultural values. It was far easier to train new hires from other industries than to convert real estate people to the company's customer-centric values.

In Sanders's mind, customers came first and if they were satisfied, the company would be profitable, and employees would earn good compensation and be motivated. In fact, Sanders, who has been known for his ability to build successful teams, has stated that he does not judge prospective employees on the basis of their resumes. Rather, as he told the *Cornell Real Estate*

Review, "I want to judge a candidate based on how we interact in an interview. I have always had an extensive interview
process...Basically, I look for people whom I like, whom I feel
good about, and feel comfortable with. We also never engage
in compensation bidding wars—we want people who want to
come to work for what we're doing, not because we're offering
the most money."[1]

Another cultural component for LaSalle was having strong
and capable directors, people who could advise Sanders, as he
describes it, "about going ten degrees to the left or ten degrees
to the right, in terms of the business strategy." This is vitally
important advice for any entrepreneur, whether the business
is just starting up or is mature and looking to expand. Seeking out the expertise, perspective, and wisdom of others contributes meaningfully to strategy setting and decision making.
"People who think that they know everything are the most
likely to get derailed," Sanders cautions. "How do you screw
up? By not having the right board of directors. You can have
the right board of directors and still screw up, but that is generally a function of leadership. The CEO needs to have very
strong people around him...and very strong directors."

Sanders wanted directors with prior governance experience,
who knew about strategy and executive compensation. He valued directors with experience in a wide range of initiatives,
who could bring their perspectives to his real estate business,
and he sought directors who were sufficiently independent to
be honest with him when he was heading in the wrong direction. In other words, he wanted directors who would be supportive but independent.

AN EXEMPLARY BOARD

An exemplary board of directors is comprised of strong, functional teams whose members trust and yet challenge one another, engaging directly with executives on critical issues facing the company. Characteristics that effective boards share include:

- Trust and candor: Members of well-functioning boards develop mutual respect. With respect comes trust and the willingness to share difficult information. Having the same information allows members to challenge one another's conclusions cogently. Constructive discussion encourages them to adjust their views in response to intelligent questions.

- Strategic involvement in the face of CEO dismissals: CEO dismissals typically fail because boards lack the strategic understanding necessary to select the appropriate replacements or provide oversight afterward. Boards that successfully replace CEOs understand the industry and other forces behind the firm's performance before they define the skills and experiences a new CEO needs. They set realistic performance expectations, backing away from forecasts they cannot meet and instead addressing underlying problems. Finally, they provide strategic oversight to new CEOs. By fostering stability before crises develop, they decrease the chances they will have to oust a CEO.

- Willingness to challenge each other: Respect and trust don't imply the absence of disagreement. Members of effective

(continued)

31

boards embrace open dissent. The bonds among board members are strong enough to withstand clashing viewpoints and challenging questions. High-performance companies have contentious boards that regard dissent as an obligation; every subject is open for discussion. They prefer to address management directly on difficult issues.

- Interchanging roles: Effective boards require their members to play a variety of roles, which provides directors with a wider view of the business and of the alternatives available to it. In one case, a director might be asked to dig deeper into the details of a particular business, and then serve as a devil's advocate in another. Discussion is often much healthier when no one is entrenched in a particular role.

- Individual accountability: There are various methods for enforcing accountability. Some companies insist that board members visit site locations. Others require them to meet with suppliers and/or customers. The most effective enforcement mechanism is old-fashioned peer pressure. Directors who take their duties seriously, and let their fellow directors know that they are expected to do the same, are the best insurance regarding individual accountability.

Keep Success in Perspective

Reaching the pinnacle of success and reaping all the benefits that entails might appear to come with some bragging rights. However, Sanders, like many executives profiled, would rather not talk about the successes too much. "I am sort of allergic to it," he quips. Such behavior might be attributable, at least in part, to humility, good manners, and not wanting to toot one's own horn. More than that, though, it reflects ingrained thinking that is important for any entrepreneur, especially at the early stages of the business: keep success in perspective. Just because you hit a home run, don't think that will happen every time. Success is the by-product of foresight and hard work, and involves some degree of timing or even luck.

Over the years, Sanders's accomplishments included building not only one but two leading real estate firms, both of which benefited from the astuteness of the founder and his disciplined study of the industry and related business sectors. By 1989, Sanders had monetized his financial interest in LaSalle Partners and he retired the same year. In 1997, LaSalle Partners went public, with an early initial public offering (IPO) in the real estate services sector. LaSalle Partners also recognized that, in order to truly serve the global Fortune 500, it needed a worldwide presence. Rather than trying to build that presence solo, LaSalle Partners merged with a company that had European and Asian businesses, but which lacked a U.S. presence: Jones Lang Wootton, which traces its history back to 1783. In 1999, Jones Lang LaSalle was formed in what was the largest international real estate merger to date. The resulting company became (and continues to be) the leading global commercial real estate services and investment management firm. Although these milestones were achieved after Sanders left the helm, they clearly would not have happened without the founder's foresight and his ability to build a strong firm with cultural values around client service.

In 1990, Sanders moved to Santa Fe, New Mexico, and founded Security Capital Group. Initially funded with his own and institutional equity capital of $108 million, Security Capital grew to become one of the most influential real estate companies, birthing a number of REITs to provide liquidity in highly-focused real estate operating companies. The *Cornell Real Estate Review* also credits him with "inspiring today's leading real estate executives, many of them having come up through Security Capital's ranks."[2]

Early on, Sanders recognized how investing in REITs, publicly traded real estate vehicles that allow both institutions and individuals to invest in real estate, was taking hold in the industry. Here was the next opportunity for Sanders, building a series of property-specific portfolios within Security Capital, which could be individually taken public as a series of REITs. Security Capital created or developed REITs across several sectors: ProLogis, with industrial real estate properties in regional and global markets; Archstone in the residential sector, with apartment buildings in the United States and Europe; Regency Centers, a leading owner, operator, and developer of grocery-anchored and community shopping centers; and CarrAmerica Realty Corporation, which focused on office properties in key U.S. markets.

In 1997, Security Capital went public with controlling interests in leading real estate companies, both listed and unlisted. At its peak in 2000, Security Capital was the largest real estate financial services, investment, and management company in the world, with more than $26 billion in combined total assets and a financial services division that had more than $2.8 billion in assets under management.

As Sanders sees it, the best thing that happened to real

estate over the course of his career was the move from a private industry to a public-dominated one. "It is a much better industry...post-securitization, because of the quality of the management teams, the quality of the information, and the evolving oversight by the analysts," he has noted.[3] The real estate industry needed to become securitized because of what Sanders describes as an inefficient appraisal system. On a daily basis, the public markets value a REIT's portfolio and platform that leaves not much room for debate relative to validation today.

Exiting a Business and Moving On

There comes a point in the life span of every entrepreneurial venture when it's time for the next stage. Sometimes the company merges with another, as was the case with LaSalle Partners. Or, it is sold to a larger company in order to combine operations to achieve scale and allow investors to earn a return on their capital. For Security Capital, that decision point came at a difficult time: the wake of September 11, when real estate companies were under pressure due to uncertainties in the sector and deteriorating economic conditions.

At that time, Sanders had received an offer from GE Capital to buy Security Capital, which still owned several property portfolios outright and maintained significant interests in the REITs it had spun off. Negotiations continued until Security Capital agreed to a reported purchase price of $26 a share, which at the time was a 26 percent premium over its closing price the day before the deal was announced. As part of the acquisition consideration, Security Capital's holdings in Prologis were distributed to Security Capital's shareholders, in addition to the cash price per share. Total value of the sale was $4 billion in cash and stock.

As he recalled the transaction, Sanders voiced some regret. Had he kept Security Capital rather than sold it, the firm could have become one of the top two or three real estate companies in the world today. For any entrepreneur, selling the firm may bring mixed blessings: on the one hand, invested capital can be extracted and financial rewards for one's efforts realized; on the other, there is often remorse over having to let go of the founder's "brainchild," which will now be nurtured and grown by another entity. Whether it's a small family business or a global enterprise, the decision to sell can be difficult and emotionally charged for the principal. A very important takeaway for entrepreneurs is never slam the door on a deal because of ego or fear. The business landscape is littered with people who never pulled the trigger and ended up with a company that became virtually worthless.

Many successful entrepreneurs are serial business builders, taking the experiences (and some of the profits) of previous ventures and committing them to new opportunities. Although Sanders, having launched two highly successful real estate firms, could have retired quietly, he has continued to pursue opportunities in niche markets. Based on research of the fallout in the financial services/banking environment, Sanders co-founded Strategic Growth Bank Incorporated in El Paso, Texas, and he and his colleagues are aggregating lending institutions with new leadership, to focus on a new model— once again, a challenged industry sector, but a new niche strategy. Entrepreneurship is attributable to having the right DNA, but it must be complemented by the ability to recognize market opportunity and satisfy that need.

Lessons and Opportunities

Sanders's advice for others centers on two things: identifying niches and establishing the right culture. Niches that are underserved, but where dramatic change is anticipated, can become fertile ground for capitalizing on opportunities that others do not yet see. Reaping those opportunities requires a viable and relevant strategy, as well as a team that is aligned with the capabilities and cultural orientation of the organization and its goals.

For those looking to go to work for an entrepreneurial firm, Sanders has further advice: "It is very critical that you join the right company that has an outstanding strategic plan and that has a very discernible culture...where you can go to work for somebody who will be brutally candid with you and develop you...[in a] very straightforward culture or environment."

His other advice, equally applicable to entrepreneurs and to those who work for them, is to be patient when it comes to the financial rewards. "Join a company where you can get rich over fifteen years not over fifteen quarters," he adds. When the culture focuses on a longer payoff, chances are it has the right values when it comes to customer service.

Throughout his career, the scope of Sanders's vision was shaped by looking at things from all angles, which enabled him to see niches and pockets of opportunities that others did not. Moreover, he looked beyond his own business to other industries, seeking best practices that could be adapted and adopted. In this way, Sanders captured opportunities early on and then created scale as his firms expanded services and developed expertise.

The key was to be a student of the business, continually learning and developing. This enabled Sanders to not only become an innovator, but also a pioneer.

TIPS FROM THE TITANS

- Seek opportunities in niches before they become obvious to others. Ideally, you want to find a niche that is devoid of competitors and where customer demand is about to explode—potentially changing the business.
- Have a highly relevant strategy that addresses customers' critical needs. This, in turn, will promote growth potential and sustained success.
- Create a culture that allows you to execute your strategy properly.
- Surround yourself with strong advisors/directors who contribute their expertise, perspective, and wisdom. Engage in discussions that go below the surface to deeper issues.
- Know when it's time to sell or merge with another firm. It may be that you've grown the company as much as you can, or the industry demands a scale that you can't achieve alone.
- Be a student of the business. No matter how many years (or even decades) of experience you have, there is always something new to learn.

Chapter Three

Make Your Mark Outside the Mainstream

> *Don't shy away from the mainstream, but don't try to make your mark [there]. Find things that need the most help... and find a way to fix that which is broken. Make a name for yourself with things that other people are ignoring.*
>
> —Stuart Miller, CEO, Lennar Corporation

Entrepreneurs have many roads to roam; there is no single pathway to success. Common to the journey of those who are most successful is venturing off the proverbial beaten track. In a world that has become more competitive and increasingly driven by consumer desires, entrepreneurs must find new and creative ways to serve the needs and satisfy the wants of their customers. Innovation and invention are crucial, particularly when staying one step ahead of the marketplace and anticipating future demands (think of the iPhone or the Segway personal transport). But a more mature business can also position itself on the cutting edge by doing things in a new or improved way.

As an entrepreneur, you do not necessarily have to invent an entirely new category of product to make your mark outside the mainstream. Sometimes it just takes looking at the familiar or the established with a fresh eye.

Building a home is hardly a new concept. Indeed, dwellings have been around as long as humankind. The modern home-building market is mature, and product differentiation may not be as pronounced as in other industries, such as consumer products and technology. Yet innovation is still critical. When it comes to consumer desires, a home is an embodiment of physical and emotional needs, from safety and security to ambiance and personal expression. Stuart Miller, CEO of Lennar Corporation, the second largest home builder in the United States, has differentiated his company by listening closely to customers and providing new features in ways that are meaningful and sustainable.

Miller did not start his company from scratch. Instead, he built upon the organization started by his father, Leonard, who founded Lennar Corporation in 1954. After succeeding his father as president and CEO in 1997, Miller has grown the company in new markets, with an enhanced product line and with a different management style, while never undermining or changing its legacy of excellence and integrity. Like other titans interviewed, Miller followed in his father's footsteps, but also charted his own course. Through his leadership, the younger Miller has elevated Lennar amid a crowded field of home builders and solidified the firm's presence during challenging times in the housing market.

Managing the Father–Son Dynamic

A substantial number of entrepreneurs get their start in a family business. This is not without its special challenges, which include balancing both the parent–child and the business relationship. Sometimes the issues are generational, reflective of the normal maturation process of pulling away and differentiating one's self from one's parents. Add a business strategy to the mix, and the dynamic becomes complicated (as anyone who has ever worked closely with a parent can attest).

In the case of Miller and his father, the working relationship was bolstered by genuine respect on both sides. "My dad was a self-made guy. He built his own company from scratch," Miller said with admiration. "His was the rags to riches story. My father had a desire to provide for his kids [Miller is the oldest of three children] those things that he did not have as a kid himself."

Having grown up in the business, Miller spent many of his early years learning every aspect of it, starting with summers while he was an undergraduate student at Harvard University and before he went to law school at the University of Miami. "I have done every job in this company and, from early on, I concluded in my mind that I wanted to work for, and perhaps ultimately oversee, the business that my father had started and had done an admirable job of creating," Miller said.

Although Miller's path into the family business was clear, he delayed joining the firm full time by going to law school. In addition to receiving an excellent advanced education, he also readied himself for the challenges he anticipated would come from being "the boss's son" and for the way people would view him in that regard. In hindsight, he acknowledged his concerns may have been more about his expectations of what could happen than the actual experience. Nonetheless, after three years in law school, he emerged with the maturity and self-confidence to enter the business world and join the family firm.

Based on his personal experiences, Miller shared a perspective for other entrepreneurs who may be entering or taking over a family business: "I don't care if it's a small local business, a bigger regional business, or a big national; for any young person to walk into an ongoing business, it is intimidating to think about the prospect of one day running it." That feeling, however, can engender qualities from humility to inquisitiveness, which can enhance leadership over the long run. As Miller observed, "In fact, what makes for good leadership and good management is not the ability to inherit something as a birthright, but instead navigate the ladder: the step-by-step ladder of being involved in all the elements and facets of a business."

Miller's personal experience of learning the ropes of the business anchored for him the importance of lifelong learning. "With the education of an undergraduate, I find it is less important what you major in, and more important that you find a passion for learning," he said. Miller added with a smile that he never took a business class ("I don't really even know what they teach you in business school"), and considers what one gets out of one's education to be much more meaningful than the particular coursework. "What I got out of my educational experience, all the way through law school, was the ability to navigate, to adapt, to do things whether I liked them or I didn't; to develop a passion for achievement. That was a big influencer for me," he said.

Early on, Miller also gained perspective on how to manage a father–son relationship within the context of a demanding family business. Although there was some friction, which was only natural, Miller credited his father for being very tactful. "When we enter our fathers' businesses as the sons, there is somewhat of a mismatch—the natural instinct that says you need to outdo your father, which turns into somewhat of a competitive engagement where the playing field is terribly uneven... It set up for some very tough conflicts with someone whom I happen to like and I happen to admire."

One particular family ritual, though, helped to smooth the waters between father and son. The elder Miller owned a small boat and took the family for outings every Sunday. "Even when we were locked in mortal combat in the company, every Sunday we would get on that boat and we would chitchat. It was kind of a wacky thing, but the conflicts between the generations can be very bruising, very heated, and the threads of the underlying relationship can either hold together or break apart. And in our case, we held together."

Measured strictly by the numbers, Lennar Corporation grew more and performed better under the younger Miller than his father. But he is quick to credit his father with having the more significant accomplishments. "There is no question in my mind that what he did was much bigger, more substantial, and more difficult," he added. "Making the first $1 million is a lot harder than making the next $10 million."

Generational Differences in Leadership

As Miller took on more responsibility in the company, he wielded more influence in setting strategy and adapting Lennar to the evolving tastes of consumers. It was a natural progression, from one generation to the next, which differentiated Miller's approach and his leadership from his father's. For example, Miller described his father as being very focused on quality and the economics side of the business, such as buying land at the right price and building homes efficiently. "But those were not the days of customer-conscious companies," he said. "So Lennar was extremely well regarded from a quality standpoint, but it wasn't driven by customer feedback." Later, when Miller took over, a customer-centric approach became a top priority for the company, without sacrificing its legacy of quality, efficiency, and economics.

As he worked closely with his father, Miller was able to appreciate his father's strengths, as well as his weaknesses. On the plus side, the elder Miller willingly and purposefully surrounded himself with people who had strengths that were different from his—the hallmark of a confident, mature leader. On the other side, Miller observed his father as an "intense controller of everything and everyone," who believed that every decision had to go through him. "That was a very limiting factor for him...You need to be able to surround yourself with people who have skills that might be different than yours and liberate them to be able to act in some kind of cultural setting of what you do and don't do."

Having one person—even if it is the founder/business owner who presumably knows the operation the best—make all the decisions becomes a bottleneck that limits progress and thwarts the development of the team. "In effect, he and I grew to be very different managers," Miller reflected. "He was completely controlling and I think I am a very good delegator. I think I learned that by watching him, and I learned what I didn't want to do."

At the same time, there were qualities that Miller inherited from his father, whether by nature or nurture, that positively influenced his leadership: "Things like integrity, focus on cash, focus on the best times, don't get carried away, and don't lose sight that the worst times are around the corner," he says.

During the most recent housing downturn, these lessons—all legacies from his father—were tested and their stellar worth was proven once again.

For any business, change is the only way to remain relevant. That might involve the generational passing of the baton or fresh talent being brought into the firm. Even when the process does not go smoothly, or there are hurt feelings and upsets on either side, these changes are necessary to the evolution of an enterprise. To understand the impact on his father, Miller tried to see things as he did: as the company founder whose son just joined the management ranks. "You are incredibly successful and your ideas have gone pretty well for a lot of years, and then here comes this new kid on the block, your son, with a different group of ideas—and some of mine were probably not the best ideas and some of mine were really good—[that sets up] a struggle between the generations," he observes.

What helped was having more "independent people" from outside the family in the company, people who provided new perspectives and created a kind of buffer that allowed both father and son to act more autonomously than they otherwise would have. In any entrepreneurial business, a deeper and more diverse bench of talent brings complementary skills and unique strengths that benefit the organization as a whole. "Don't worry that someone might be smarter or stronger; enable them to be smarter and stronger," Miller added. "Revel in the greatness of others, because the component parts of anything make the whole really strong. Then everybody is successful."

Although they had understandable differences at work and even in management styles, Miller and his father, who passed away in 1992, remained very close. Looking back, Miller spoke with obvious pride for the "incredible foundation" that his father established, having built a company "by sheer brute force of personality and perseverance."

His respect for his father's accomplishments was underscored by an appreciation of the knowledge and insight that the elder Miller possessed by virtue of a unique set of life experiences. Not even an Ivy League education could match it. Top of the list of lessons Miller learned from his father was "everything must be done with absolute integrity."

Putting Integrity Above Expediency

It is a fact of life that, at some point, all businesses face their share of troubles. The difficulties may be related to the economy or a new competitor in the marketplace. A product launch may be less than successful, or an existing offering may suddenly be viewed as outmoded. Whatever the challenge, how the company and its leadership act in response telegraphs a powerful message internally and externally. Entrepreneurs can never lose sight of the old saying that a reputation takes a lifetime to build but can be lost in a day. Miller witnessed integrity in action by observing the way his father navigated difficulties. "Those lessons have probably stayed with me the longest," he remarks.

When he joined the company full time in 1982, the housing market was in the doldrums, having suffered through a recession in the early 1980s that had left a lingering economic malaise. In order to battle persistent inflation, the prime interest rate had been ratcheted higher, eventually reaching 21.5 percent in June 1982, which hardly made it an attractive time to be a home builder. Although Lennar Corporation had an inventory of unsold properties, the elder Miller never shifted the properties back to the lenders, which would have damaged the company's reputation and undermined its relationship with customers. Instead, he stayed true to the loan terms and made timely payments.

Leadership mettle is tested during the tough times, when the expedient response appears to be to dump assets and run away or to renege on promises. True leaders, however, uphold their commitments, thus establishing a line in the sand with regard to business ethics and culture. It's no surprise that the companies that hold themselves to higher standards are often those that fare better when the turnaround materializes and conditions improve.

By the mid-1980s, Lennar Corporation had about fifteen hundred vacant condominiums in various properties, and the condo market "had fallen off the cliff." Miller took it upon himself to pursue an innovative solution to the problem, surprising even his father when it was successful. He packaged about nine hundred of the condos together, leased them, and then sold them to a syndicator in bulk: a $46 million deal that, for a relatively small company at the time, was a significant transaction. By getting out from under those properties, Lennar was able to improve the way it was perceived by lenders and also by the marketplace.

For Miller, the experience confirmed his instincts and also taught him a valuable lesson: not to get into a crowded field such as the condominium market just because everyone else was there. The real value to be realized was in "tackling the things that were not crowded and that were maybe even neglected." Miller called this approach "walking in the back door" in order to draw less attention, particularly during the test phase, which would lead to another lesson from the entrepreneurial journey: be a pioneer, but slowly.

THE RIGHT LEADER FOR THE RIGHT TIME

Leaders come in all styles and approaches, from visionary innovators who generate the next best idea to those who are able to methodically implement a plan and measure performance. Leaders often have a broad skill set, but typically they display true competency in a few major areas.

A serial entrepreneur is probably not the best person for an existing company in need of a turnaround, nor is someone with expertise in reengineering a firm likely to be best suited for a start-up. It's a question of fit.

To attract, retain, and develop top talent with the right skill set for the company, boards and corporate leaders must be discerning about the organization's needs and the challenges that must be addressed. As companies go through cycles—from rapid growth to consolidation—the talent bench is provided with key experiences that build their competence and confidence to meet future demands.

The Methodical Pioneer

As promising as a new venture or idea appears, enthusiasm that might tempt you to jump in without sufficient due diligence needs to be tempered with a well-thought-out approach. Although the entrepreneur is always on the lookout for new ideas, these ideas must be thoroughly vetted. "Pioneering needs to be done methodically, slowly, and carefully. There is no limit to the amount of testing to be done," Miller advised.

For Lennar, new product innovation often involves new

technologies for home design and development, as well as for home use, from the way a house is constructed to amenities that appeal to consumers. "We are very careful about the testing process," Miller said. "There can be countless things incorporated into all kinds of products, and in homes in particular, that can give rise to long-term problems if you are not careful."

Patience is an odd quality for entrepreneurs, almost to the point of being oxymoronic. To be on the cutting edge requires being constantly on the lookout for new opportunities and thinking 24–7 about how to advance the business. At the same time, you must have the discipline to pick a few of the best ideas and execute them with precision. This can create huge tension for the entrepreneurial spirit, for whom there is usually no dearth of new ideas. The inability to prioritize and then implement the best, however, is the downfall of many entrepreneurs, and becomes the major drawback that will keep them from reaching the pinnacle of success and becoming a titan.

Thus, for the entrepreneur, it is a balancing act between constant innovation and staying aligned with core competencies; improving on a product while not giving up the features that consumers value. Even if these challenges are handled perfectly, not every new idea will be successful. A classic example is the Edsel, a sedan manufactured by Ford Motor Company in the late 1950s. The car never gained popularity with buyers, costing the company millions of dollars. In the process, American business vernacular gained a word synonymous with product flop: Edsel. (*Time* magazine, in a commemoration of the "50 Worst Cars of All Time," noted the Edsel was "kind of homely, fuel thirsty and too expensive, particularly at the outset of the late '50s recession." In addition, it was the "first victim of Madison Avenue hyper-hype," making promises to consumers that just weren't delivered.[1])

A company cannot be so scared about potential failure, though, that it fails to innovate (which would, in fact, be the greater failure). "I have had some fabulous failures in my business career and anybody who is doing something new and different has failures," Miller said. "I advise others as I advise my children, to embrace [their failures]. Make sure that you're not afraid to look them in the eye, even though they might hurt in a moment in time. See them for what they are because they are your best learning experiences."

Miller recalled one particular failure in the mid-1990s involving a "home of the future" with voice-activated technology, which really captured the attention of buyers. After the product was tested, Lennar believed it was a compelling offering that could differentiate the company in the marketplace. Unfortunately, when the technology was installed in homes, it failed. The small subset of testing had not provided enough variation of experiences to predict accurately what consumers could encounter—or what havoc could be wreaked by the vagaries of nature.

The technology was supposed to allow a consumer to walk into her home and activate certain features with spoken commands such as "lights on" or "TV." Unfortunately, thunderstorms would sometimes interfere with the system, and lights would turn on unexpectedly in the middle of the night. Looking back, the situation was somewhat comical, but in the midst of it, Lennar had to deal with some frustrated and upset customers. The company took the high road, removing the technology and compensating consumers. At the end of this difficult episode, Miller found a valuable lesson to learn and apply the next time: "We probably rushed a little bit too much to market with something we felt was a game changer."

The experience did not dissuade Lennar in the least from its drive toward continued innovation. Today, in fact, it offers improved voice-activation technology in its homes. ("It works a hundred times better now than when we introduced the stuff," Miller noted.) In the business world, making "excellent mistakes"—or, as Miller calls them, "fabulous failures"—is an expected and inevitable part of the innovation learning curve, without which a business will most likely plateau and then tumble.

More recently, the entire home-building industry, and, indeed, the economy as a whole, has suffered a dramatic down-turn that has left virtually no company unscathed. Lennar, like its peers, has suffered its share of lumps and losses as the market corrects. Yet even here, Miller retains his perspective and sees even severe problems as learning opportunities. "As I say to our people...as mistakes that we have made have been revealed by market conditions or other things, let's not shy away from them," he said. "We have lost money and that is our tuition. Make sure that we don't go through school paying the tuition and then be afraid to use the education. Let's learn from it and make sure that we incorporate that as part of a rich learning experience."

The Internal Game of Entrepreneurship

Throughout our conversation, Miller exhibited a high degree of self-knowledge. Introspection is an important quality for any leader, especially the entrepreneur who needs to balance the drive to build a business and become a market leader with the discipline of knowing when to get out of the way. Miller demonstrated his inward focus when contemplating what his career might have looked like had he taken a different path. "I think that people who are in my shoes would love to say of themselves, 'Had I been born in a different setting, I would have been just as good, just as strong, just as innovative,' but I don't know that I could really convince myself that this is the truth," he commented. "I certainly was born with a set of opportunities and, frankly, I will never know how I might have harvested a different set of opportunities and how my career might have gone differently."

Miller offered the example of the so-called butterfly effect, the concept that even a small change (e.g., a butterfly beating its wings in one part of the world) can cause a tremendous shift or change in another (a hurricane that is spawned in another part of the world). Similarly, even a small difference in his life could have dramatically altered the outcome of his career. The point is moot because his path into the family company was set at an early age. What he is certain of, however, are the advantages he gained early in life, not just materially, but also emotionally and in terms of development, thanks to his father and the foundation he established.

The success of Lennar Corporation began with Leonard Miller, who established a legacy of quality, value, and integrity. Later, when his son, Stuart Miller, joined the firm and climbed the corporate ladder, the company grew with the times. Along the way, Miller father and son have shepherded a firm that continues to be distinguished by values that will outlive and outlast any one individual.

MAKE YOUR MARK OUTSIDE THE MAINSTREAM

TIPS FROM THE TITANS

- ☛ Don't avoid the mainstream, but make your mark away from the crowd.
- ☛ Honor the legacy of the past, but don't be afraid to change and innovate with the times.
- ☛ Remember that the ability to learn is more important than what you already know.
- ☛ Delegate and empower others; appreciate their unique talents and contributions to the organization.
- ☛ Never compromise integrity for any reason.
- ☛ Embrace "fabulous failures" as the only way to advance along the learning curve.

Chapter Four

Grow the Bottom Line—Period

When I talk about growing a business, I always talk about the bottom line. Don't talk about the head count; don't talk about sales. It's always about after-tax profit.

—Noel Watson, Former CEO and Current Chairman of the Board, Jacobs Engineering Group Inc.

Entrepreneurs, by and large, are idea people, devising new concepts and next-generation ventures, and creating potential markets. With such an intent focus on what could be, however, they may not pay enough attention to what *is*—meaning, the hard measures of current performance. Although many start-ups are not profitable initially, for such is the nature of the beast, profitability is the difference between an idea and a viable, sustainable business. It doesn't matter how much a business appears to be growing with new stores, increased head count, or even higher sales. At the end of the day, profitability is the differentiator between an interesting concept and a business capable of going to the next level.

Measures such as profit margins and net profit hold entrepreneurs and their teams accountable to delivering the numbers. Unless they are disciplined by nature (or they surround themselves with people who are), entrepreneurs who don't watch the bottom line will likely find that the business has come off the rails. Admittedly, most entrepreneurs are not of that ilk; they are most comfortable generating possibilities and revenues. But it takes discipline and focus to realize profits consistently over the years.

Yet this is what it takes for any successful start-up, maturing business, or established enterprise: they must grow the business, advance new products, venture into new markets, improve efficiency, and take market share from competitors. There is no other way to reach the next level of maturity and sustainability.

This is the gospel of entrepreneurship and business building preached by Noel Watson, former CEO and current chairman of the board of Jacobs Engineering Group Inc., one of the world's largest and most diverse providers of professional technical services, with operations in North America, South America, Europe, the Middle East, India, Australia, Africa, and Asia. But Jacobs wasn't always a New York Stock Exchange–traded global enterprise, building dams, chemical plants, and pharmaceutical facilities and providing services to clients ranging from NASA and sovereign governments to large industrial and commercial clients. When Watson joined the company the first time, after graduating with a chemical engineering degree from the University of North Dakota in 1958, it was a small consulting firm founded by Dr. Joseph J. Jacobs.

Watson left two years later to join a large mining company (his plan all along had been to gain some experience in an operating company, as well), but he was back at Jacobs in December 1965. He spent the rest of his career there. The firm Watson returned to had about one hundred people housed in a small headquarters in Pasadena, California. Starting out in the consulting business, Jacobs focused initially on mining and minerals processing projects. Over the years, it expanded in size and scope, and eventually sold equipment as well as a variety of client services and solutions related to engineering and construction. By the early 1980s, its workforce numbered twenty-five hundred employees. Then a recession hit the engineering and construction sector, and the firm struggled, losing money for the first time in its history. Surviving and eventually thriving could only happen with a strong bottom line. "That's how we define growth at Jacobs," Watson said. "Nothing counts in the end but the bottom line."

Over the years, Watson has held various jobs at Jacobs, growing right along with the company, from a process engineer and then a project manager to, eventually, co-chief operating officer in the mid-1980s, president in 1987, and CEO in 1992. He became chairman of the board in 2004. During Watson's time as CEO, the company's revenues increased from $1.1 billion to more than $5 billion, with a corresponding increase in profits. Today, its revenues are more than $10 billion, and it employs more than sixty thousand people worldwide in more than twenty-five countries. It operates in a variety of sectors, including aerospace and defense, automotive and industrial, buildings, chemicals and polymers, consumer and forest products, energy, environmental programs, infrastructure, mining and minerals, oil and gas, pharmaceuticals and biotechnology, refining, and technology.

Looking at Jacobs today, one would hardly consider it a start-up. Yet for entrepreneurs in any sector, it offers powerful lessons in getting to the next stage of development: a mature company that grows largely through retaining market share—and taking share away from competitors. "If you don't grow the bottom line, you will not survive. The only real measurement is growing your profits. The business is either growing or dying," Watson said. "You have to be taking market share every day—somehow. Everyone would like to be a genius like Steve Jobs and create the iPhone, but there aren't many of those kinds of things happening on the face of the earth. However, there are a lot of reasonable markets out there in which to grow a business. It has to grow every day, which means you have to take a little market share from somebody every day."

The true test of an entrepreneurial firm is in the second stage, as it morphs from a start-up into a more mature company with a track record. Once a company is established on a great idea and reaches a certain level, there will be a maturation point. From here, the way forward is largely through improvement—the proverbial new "bells and whistles" that generate more revenue, improve efficiencies and profit margins, and increase profitability.

At this point in the entrepreneurial game, the real yardage to be gained on the competitive playing field is often not because of a new product with performance that's equivalent to a completed eighty-yard pass. For many companies, it's knocking out five to eight yards at a time—the slow, methodical, and incremental progress. Although this is frustrating and even boring for many entrepreneurs, who are eager to launch the next big, best thing, this is the phase that solidifies a business, polishes the model or go-to-market approach, and improves efficiencies.

Fortunately for Watson, he excelled in the second stage. "My claim to fame would be very steady growth that I presided over," he said. "That's my accomplishment. That is where I take my satisfaction."

Without such steady growth even a large, seemingly invulnerable company can become prone to declines and even bankruptcy. Back in the 1990s, when Watson was teaching a course at Jacobs College, a training and leadership development program of the company, he predicted that General Motors would go bankrupt one day. Those who heard him laughed. But no one was laughing when the unthinkable happened in June 2009, in the midst of the worst economic downturn since the Great Depression, when GM—in spite of $19.4 billion in federal help—filed for bankruptcy. "You just can't lose market share every year and survive," Watson said. "They were dying; they weren't growing."

The only antidote to such a fate is sustainable, measurable growth, which for Jacobs has been driven largely by long-term client relationships. (The company states that more than 90 percent of its work is repeat business from clients.) It credits this strategy with yielding cost advantages and better profitability.

"Everything that we have, we worked long and hard for over the years to build and grow the business," Watson said. "In most businesses, there's not a game changer. It's just slogging it out. Ninety-nine percent of the businesses in this country slog it out with somebody...I am not talking about a one- to two-year thing; this is a long-term game."

Although strategies are executed over the long term, measuring results and being accountable for them happen in the short term. "As I said, it's a very long game, but your executives [need to be held] accountable almost on a day-to-day basis,"

Watson said. "I always tell people, take care of today; tomorrow takes care of itself."

The balance between having long-term and short-term views can be tricky to manage, but as Watson states, it's critical for an entrepreneur. Problems must be addressed immediately. If a client has a need, it must be attended to right away. In these instances, procrastination is the deadliest sin. Having urgency around these priorities helps to engender an attitude of responsiveness and being accountable for what is happening now.

Over a twenty-year time frame, from the late 1980s through 2008–2009, Jacobs grew, on average, about 15 percent per year. Such growth doesn't just happen. From start-up to mature company, the only way to achieve sustainable success is by measurement. The often-quoted adage in business is "what gets measured gets managed." Watson offered a slightly different take on that axiom: "You can't improve what you don't measure." Measurement means not only the end results, but the incremental steps to achieving them—starting with the team.

Results Come from a Winning Team

It is a symbiotic relationship: a winning team is attracted to a company that is growing. And, in order to grow, a business requires a group of highly talented and competent individuals who work together. "The only way you get good people is if you are taking market share and improving profits in the long run," Watson added.

For the entrepreneur/founder, the quality of the team is a critical component to sustainability. The reason is simple: typically, the entrepreneur has the ideas to launch the business, but it takes a team with diverse yet complementary skills and talents to help take it to the next level. Again, symbiosis plays a role: talented people want to do exciting, challenging work—and that requires a talented team to build a book of business, meaning projects in the pipeline. As Watson observed, "You need to have work on the table, and it must be good work. It needs to be things that people are interested in. Then you have to go and get the best people out there to do the work."

Having the "best team" in Watson's eyes doesn't just depend on the internal talent pool. He looks at "the best that's out there," including in markets outside the United States where Jacobs also operates. "If you are going to be a global company, that means you've got to have the best guys in France, the best guys in Italy, and the best guys in the Middle East," he explained. "And to do that, you've got to have a really global attitude, which means that these guys all have a chance for the brass ring.... I argue hard that a company isn't global until it is run by somebody who wasn't born and raised in the country of origin."

In Watson's estimation, when it comes to taking market share and converting it into future opportunities, about 70 percent of success depends upon the people and about 30 percent on the sales strategy. Clearly, going to market requires having the best team to be successful. If a project or potential client is an A-list prospect, then the talent going after that opportunity must be the best there is.

"People talk about A, B, and C teams, I have to laugh. I have never sold anything in my life except with an A team. The buyers are too smart to buy anything but from an A team," Watson said. "When you're pitching a big government [for a project], you have to recognize that they know talent when they see it. If you show up with the best team, you will win—maybe not all the time, but most of the time. If you show up with a team that isn't the best, it's very hard to win."

For entrepreneurs in any business, losing out on a bid for a project or not being chosen by a potential new client results in a postmortem to figure out what went wrong. Although the possible explanations are as varied as the opportunities themselves, the reason may come down to the strength of the competitor's team.

Talent development means holding onto the good performers. Measure and reward based on metrics, so that people are accountable. At the same time, people develop differently. Some are strong right out of the gate; others mature more slowly, while making steady progress. Whatever the pace of development, people clearly make the difference, and having a team of talented individuals is a competitive advantage.

How individuals are developed and rewarded also reflects the corporate culture. A positive environment is one in which people are given opportunities to be challenged and to develop new skills and competencies, are treated respectfully, and are rewarded with a share of the profits. Equally important is a path for advancement, so that bright, talented people can manage their careers. If there is nowhere for them to go, they will take their knowledge and experience elsewhere and become part of someone else's team.

Discipline

Ask entrepreneurs about their most valued attributes and the answers you'll probably hear most often are qualities such as creativity and vision. This is absolutely correct. Entrepreneurs see potential and possibility where others do not or cannot. But there is another trait as important as the ability to dream a new venture into being: discipline.

Discipline encompasses the necessary strength, courage, and determination to keep the business moving forward by taking a hard look at things (especially, as mentioned earlier, at profitability). In my work with entrepreneurs and business leaders across every industry and type of company, from innovative start-ups to mature leaders in their fields, discipline is a defining characteristic.

Watson credits his father, who owned a small business, as a mentor who valued common sense (which Watson called the most important ingredient to getting along in life) and discipline. "I was taught discipline very early on," he added. "I was taught to use my head to make judgments."

Another strong influence was company founder Dr. Joseph J. Jacobs. Analogous to the father–son dynamic explored in earlier chapters (Bill Marriott in chapter 1 and Stuart Miller in chapter 3), Watson and Dr. Jacobs's relationship represented a similar generational span. In selecting and grooming Watson and ultimately turning the reins of the company over to him, Dr. Jacobs demonstrated the all-important success trait among entrepreneurs who reach titan status: recognizing and attracting strong talent and retaining and developing it.

THE SEAMLESS TRANSITION

A common challenge for many companies, particularly when it comes to succession, is managing the handoff, making it a seamless transition rather than a contest between two competitors.

(continued)

Because of the competitive spirit of many successors, disagreements with the CEO can be perceived as contests to be won. Unfortunately, focusing on immediate conflicts can cause the successor to lose sight of the ultimate goal: to move to the top and lead the company forward.

Successors must know when to pull back and how to do it gracefully. One way for the successor to keep his emotions in check is to practice empathy and focus on what the current CEO is going through, rather than on his own experience. Successors need to remember that, increasingly, CEOs struggle with losing the position that gave them a strong sense of identity.

Perhaps the most critical—and most difficult—part of managing the successor's dilemma is allowing the CEO to save face. In many situations, a successor is well advised to let a CEO's pride win, which may mean losing the battle, but ultimately winning the war.

As he looked to recruit others to his team, Watson put a lot of stock in discipline and focus as crucial qualities. "We can sit around and dream about tomorrow, dream about next year, and dream about what if, but you've got to have a [team] that works," he said. "It takes a lot of energy [along with] focus and discipline and a reasonably decent brain."

Numeric by nature, Watson demonstrated a strong discipline and work ethic that he applied to the study of the business. Much of the work he did early on revolved around discounted cash flow, which is akin to measuring the lifeblood and health of the company. Then, as Jacobs expanded globally, applying that same discipline allowed the company to judge acquisitions on the basis of their fundamentals—not just the appearance of opportunities to be tapped. "We looked at the synergies. We looked at whether we really wanted to be in that market," Watson explained.

His disciplined approach offers an important lesson for entrepreneurs who, at some point in the growth cycle of their companies, may very well be faced with the opportunity to expand through an acquisition or merger. No deal should be undertaken just for the sake of doing a deal (although the temptation may be there to do just that). The decision of whether to acquire another firm or to merge to create a larger entity must be made on a disciplined, bottom-line basis, so that one plus one is more than just two. Without the right complementary strengths (especially culture and leadership mind-set) and synergies, the deal could end up being subtractive—not additive.

Jacobs's expansion through globalization occurred in response to client needs. Its first operation outside the United States was in Ireland, where Jacobs had worked on a pharmaceutical project. When clients approached the firm in the early 1990s about building operations elsewhere in Europe, because of the promise of the European Union to open markets and promote cross-border commerce, Jacobs needed to operate beyond Ireland. The answer was to acquire a British entity with three offices in the United Kingdom and a small operation in India. Although the acquired company was "losing money hand over fist," as Watson recalled, the real value was in the expanded global footprint—and the confidence that Jacobs could improve the profitability, which it did.

That is not to say that every acquisition Jacobs made was a success. In fact, Watson called one an "unmitigated disaster" (although he offered no further details). Most important in retrospect was the attitude and ability to learn the lessons and move on. "I rode through it and said, 'Let's try not to do that again, and let's get on with it,' " Watson recalled.

In contrast with some perfectionists in the organization, Watson was described as being more of a "hip shooter"— although clearly this disciplined, numbers guy was careful and methodical in his approach. The differentiator, however, could very well be his ability to move on and not become psyched out by having made a mistake. His attitude holds an important lesson for entrepreneurs who want to learn from mistakes. Once the meaning and the takeaway from the experience have been identified and digested, it is time to move forward. Being haunted by past errors and missteps can cripple a leader and a company because it leads to an inordinate amount of second-guessing and doubts. It takes maturity in leadership to realize that not every move is going to be a winner (although, with due diligence and careful study, you hope to have as high a success rate as possible). And it takes wisdom and experience to remember and learn from mistakes, while not being hampered by them.

No One Size Fits All for Leaders

With a long and successful career spent almost exclusively at one company, Watson has an enviable perspective. He witnessed the growth of a company from one hundred to more than sixty thousand employees, and from one small headquarters in Pasadena to more than two hundred offices globally. Looking back, Watson joked that he "never had a good idea in my life." In the next breath, he added, "But I sure recognized them when they go by."

Watson's observation speaks to the differences in leadership that exist across industries and even within companies. Not everyone can be—or needs to be—a visionary capable of creating the next Google or Apple Computer. Genius is found not only at the whiteboard spewing the next generation of ideas. It is also found among those who, like Watson, take a disciplined and methodical approach to evaluating possibilities and measuring results.

"I have had the good fortune to have a lot of business contacts. And I have to tell you that great leaders come in all sizes and shapes," Watson said. "Some of them are charismatic as all get out, and some of them are just really good at what they do. Some of them have communication skills that are mind-boggling."

To be a successful entrepreneur and even become a titan one day, you must recognize your own inherent strengths, talents, and weaknesses, and seek complementary skills for your team. Although everyone can learn and develop additional skills, people tend to revert to their strengths. Fortunately, there is room for everyone and a need for a variety of strengths within an organization.

One common truth that cuts across all ventures and opportunities is the need to focus on the bottom line. Without profitability, there is no future. All the good ideas in the world will come to naught if there is no well-tuned engine in place to drive the business forward. Dream and plan, yes, but also measure and hold accountable. It is a time-tested recipe for entrepreneurial success.

TIPS FROM THE TITANS

- Rely on hard measures—e.g., profit margins and profitability. Remember, in the end, nothing counts but the bottom line.
- Grow the business by gaining market share, which often (particularly in a mature sector) means taking it from others through better efficiency, service, and pricing.
- Attract a winning team who can further the goals of a growing business, which, in turn, will attract talented people.
- Develop and hone discipline, which for the creative, idea-generating entrepreneur is critical to taking the business to the next level.
- Learn from mistakes, but don't become distracted and derailed by them.

Chapter Five

Coach, Mentor, and Teach Others

> *I do consider myself a teacher, and that started early on. My parents were teachers. I would consider them, especially my father, to be the earliest role models for the importance of teaching. As I got older and entered the workforce and began to manage people, the importance of teaching not only became obvious, but I began to develop my own style.*
>
> —Julia Stewart, Chairman and CEO, DineEquity, Inc.

Truth be told, not many entrepreneurs are known for being great coaches and mentors who devote a good deal of their time transferring skills and knowledge. Most of them, and understandably so, are impatient. They don't suffer fools gladly, and those who can't keep up with them are regarded as better off getting out of the way. With a tendency to be demanding and impatient, an entrepreneur—particularly during the "do or die" early stages of a company—has a million things to focus on. Being a teacher usually isn't one of them.

There is a point in the development of the entrepreneur and of the organization, however, when coaching and mentoring become vitally important. A company cannot scale on the talent and know-how of just one person or a small group of insiders. As the business matures and expands—such as with a franchise operation that must literally replicate itself countless times over—others need to embrace and possess the same knowledge and expertise. At this point, the entrepreneur must develop a new slate of competencies as well: that of the coach, mentor, and teacher.

Julia Stewart, chairman and CEO of DineEquity, Inc., acquired this perspective early in life. Her parents were both high school teachers, and she credits them—and in particular her father—as being role models who demonstrated the importance of coaching and mentoring others. "That has served me well throughout my career. I do consider myself, in many ways, to be a teacher," Stewart observed.

Other lessons learned early in her career focused on what it truly means to manage and lead others. To Stewart, to lead is to serve, which requires earning the respect and trust of direct reports and colleagues. It is also a perspective she gained through her interactions with others, such as Carl Karcher, founder of Carl's Jr.; Kyle Craig, former executive vice president at Burger King; and John Martin, former president of Taco Bell. "Throughout my career, there have been people who supported me, and that was invaluable," she continued. "They showed me that it is a privilege to lead others and to take that responsibility seriously—to make it an important part of who you are."

Stewart is best known for revitalizing the iconic restaurant chain International House of Pancakes (IHOP) and then acquiring the much larger Applebee's and turning it around as well. Her view of the business, however, did not start at the top, although she spent many years as an executive in well-known chains—Carl's Jr., Burger King, Stuart Anderson's Black Angus Cattle Company Restaurants, Taco Bell, and Applebee's. She joined IHOP in 2001 and became the CEO in 2002, and took on the additional role of chairman of the board in 2006. Rather, Stewart, who earned a bachelor's degree in communications from San Diego State University, first learned the restaurant business as a sixteen-year-old, waiting tables at a local IHOP. After working at a steakhouse chain and then for an advertising agency (the result of winning a marketing contest for McDonald's while in college), she met Carl Karcher on an airplane, and he convinced her to return to the restaurant business—she's been there ever since.

As Stewart told her story with warmth and enthusiasm, she noted with equal good humor that her career path had not followed her parents' first choice for her. Not surprisingly, as both taught high school, they encouraged Stewart to become a teacher. In time, however, Stewart was able to help her father, in particular, to see that her profession was more aligned with his dreams for her than he realized. "When I was at Taco Bell, I finally got him to spend a day with me. We went around and toured Taco Bells all day. He got to see me—and by then, I was a fairly senior executive, running a lot of the country operationally—in action. He watched me go into the restaurants and coach and mentor," Stewart recalled. "Finally, after all of that...he said, 'I get what you have been trying to say to me all of these years. You *do* teach; you just don't do it in a classroom. You do it in the kitchen of a restaurant. You *do* mentor and you *do* coach. You are making differences in [employees'] lives. And I couldn't be more proud of you.'"

For Stewart and her father, it was a moment of shared epiphany. Clearly, for her father, the realization that his daughter was a teacher, just without the formalities of the title and classroom, helped him to appreciate her leadership and the way she served others in the organization. For Stewart, arguably, the moment solidified what her goal had been all along: to lead others by elevating their skills, knowledge, and confidence in executing the strategy and improving customer service. Later, as the head of a casual dining chain, she would use those teaching skills to bring others on board as part of a challenging turnaround and to integrate a significant acquisition.

Working the Plan

Entrepreneurs, as stated in earlier chapters, are idea generators. Getting a concept off the whiteboard and making it reality, however, takes buy-in. No matter how much the entrepreneur believes in the potential and sees the possibilities, if others do not share that vision, a business won't get off the ground. This fact of entrepreneurial life applies to turnarounds as well as start-ups. In the former scenario, there may be widespread concern, fear, apathy, and a host of other emotions associated with a business in trouble. Therefore, getting people to commit to do the work (and, often, to accept the necessary sacrifices such as head-count reductions and doing more with and for less) is the only way forward.

When Stewart joined IHOP, the chain was in need of revitalization. She implemented significant shifts in strategy; for example, she transformed the company into a pure-play franchisor. Along the way, IHOP also realized its goal to become number one in family dining. Her vision and collaboration, along with a good deal of toughness, earned her the nickname among her franchisees of the "Velvet Hammer." As she told the *New York Times* in a 2007 interview, "What that means is…I am tough on standards and raising the bar, but I do it in a caring manner.…I'm very supportive. My style is much more collaborative, to do it in a relationship-building way."[1]

Stewart's combination of being tough on standards but supportive with people presents a model for other entrepreneurs, whether they are in franchise businesses or are trying to roll out a strategy across a company. High expectations and strict measures when it comes to performance set the bar appropriately high, while collaboration combined with teaching and mentoring help people to achieve or even surpass the goals and targets. Thus, it becomes a win–win for the organization and for the team.

As Stewart told the *Times*, "It is a different set of skills to run a franchise organization. No one [among the owners] reports to me. These are all very successful businessmen and women who have an entrepreneurial spirit, which I really admire and respect, but yet they want the leadership and direction from us as the franchisor. It's a fine line you walk in providing leadership and direction and strategy and tools, but doing it in a way where it is a push–pull."

As Stewart explained in our conversation, success in the IHOP turnaround required "working the plan" and sharing it widely across the organization. "I'm a big believer in taking people with you," Stewart explained. "A really good example is when I first came to IHOP. I spent six months, touring the country…and talking to franchisees. [I asked them], 'What do you think is working? What's not?'"

After gathering input, she finalized a plan and rolled it out to others—or, as Stewart called it, "socialized it" with the board of directors, employees, franchisees, vendor partners, and

THE WISDOM OF TITANS

shareholders. "It was this notion of working the plan, of having a very clear vision, of getting everybody to buy in, all the way down to the food server," she added. "We now have almost 250,000 employees who either work for us or our franchisees. So getting people to buy into the plan and then work it is critical."

Successful business leaders tend to be strong on communication, enabling them to connect with others emotionally and intellectually. The takeaway for any entrepreneur is the importance of not only devising a plan that works, but also getting others to buy in and work it.

Success Through Others

In a franchise organization such as IHOP, the point is clear: success comes through others. These owners are not employees who can be directed. These are independent business-people who must be guided, informed, and coached on how to execute the plan. As a friend who was an executive in the restaurant industry once told Stewart, "I couldn't do what you do...I get up every morning and I tell people what to do. You get up every morning and you counsel, you suggest, you impact, you influence...."

Although many entrepreneurs will not be in a franchise environment, the lesson applies when it comes to making the transition from directing to mentoring. In a small start-up, an entrepreneur can get away with having a strong hand on the wheel, being the proverbial captain who gives the orders to the crew. Even when there is a need for consensus, there are simply not that many people to convince. As a company gets bigger, however, there are more decision makers and influencers. The entrepreneur cannot be the only one in charge. At the second stage, having transitioned from a start-up to a more established company, gaining the trust, acceptance, and cooperation of others who hold responsibility in the company is huge. Unfortunately, this is a transition that many entrepreneurs cannot make, and this failure stifles their ability to become titans of much larger and more successful enterprises.

One way to ease that transition is to purposefully build a team of the best talent (as Noel Watson of Jacobs Engineering explained in chapter 4). Strong and capable people may need to be "sold" on the merits of a plan, but once they commit, they bring the sum total of their talents and experience to bear. "I always [told] myself that I am going to surround myself with the brightest and best people and earn their respect and loyalty. They are going to be far brighter in their field than I can ever hope to be," Stewart said. "And I am so blessed that I have surrounded myself with the best and brightest who are far smarter than I am."

In this way, the leader not only becomes the teacher—but also the student. "I will say to them, 'Teach me, educate me, coach me, and help me [know] how you got this answer. Then let's work together and go make the moon and stars," she added.

This is a habit that Stewart developed early in her career when she was learning all she could about the restaurant business. She sought out those who would willingly invest their time to explain what they knew and how they approached things. As she moved up in the organization and became a leader, Stewart never stopped asking people for their input.

THE TEACHING LEADER

As corporate leaders and boards of directors seek to develop talent as part of a succession plan, grooming candidates for top roles in the company, a key quality to look for is the ability to lead others by coaching and mentoring. Leaders at every level of the organization, including the CEO, need to spend a significant portion of their time developing others. This includes identifying development needs and purposefully providing opportunities to learn and gain experience.

A "teaching leader" is also a servant leader, putting the needs of others first. Whenever buy-in and consensus are critical, a leader who can connect and communicate becomes a real asset. The goal is to demonstrate, by words and actions, a sincere attitude that "we're all in this together."

When a company is in a turnaround situation, it's common for employees to have doubts. Things are troubled and challenging, and people naturally wonder about the viability of any plan. They may even harbor questions about the leader's ability to pull off a badly needed revitalization or rescue a faltering company. Therefore, the leader needs the ability to earn the trust and respect of others so that others believe. The leader must instill the confidence that she can make a difference, thus inspiring others to commit to the plan.

Owning Mistakes

The paradox here is that the more vulnerable a leader is willing to be, the stronger she is apt to be perceived. This is especially true for entrepreneurs who, after driving change and pushing

76

ideas and plans into practice, need to establish a culture in which people can try—and sometimes fail. The best way to do that is for the leader to admit to the organization when she's made a mistake. This ability is a differentiator between those who can become titans and those who remain serial entrepreneurs, launching start-ups but never personally taking a company to the next level.

When Stewart was first named to lead IHOP and effect a turnaround, she had a very ambitious agenda. Also like many new leaders eager to make their mark quickly—to put those points up on the board in short order—she moved at an aggressive pace. Soon enough, she started hearing from franchisees, who didn't disagree with the priorities and what needed fixing, only with her pacing and sequencing. Stewart shared the insight with her management team and confided that she felt the franchisees had a valid point. To a person, her team pushed back, saying it would be a terrible mistake—nothing less than a sign of weakness. They urged staying the course; to them, being strong meant not blinking, let alone backing down.

After some reflection, Stewart advised her team that not only was she going to listen to the franchisees and adapt the plan accordingly, she was going to apologize that she hadn't listened more carefully sooner. Needless to say, the team thought these were the worst possible steps, from which she would never recover as a leader. The reality proved different. Almost immediately after communicating her apology and decision to all franchisees, they began calling and writing to Stewart personally—surprised and, of course, pleased that their feedback had been heard and taken seriously, and bowled over by her admission and apology. Along with expressions of gratitude, the franchisees communicated their commitments to be open-minded and honest in their dealings with her. Stewart, who had never experienced anything like it before in her career of working with franchisees, had set the tone for a constructive relationship that continues with those franchisees (and others) more than a decade later.

The lesson here is that no one (including the corner office occupants) has a monopoly on good ideas and the right thing to do. In fact, by virtue of making it to the top, one has to listen even more closely and acknowledge the obstacles that can get in the way of receiving the best information. And, of course, admitting to human frailty and apologizing shows strength of character and self-awareness—not weakness.

Hand in hand with owning the mistakes is showing appreciation for the efforts of others. In a fast-paced, highly competitive environment, such things can easily become overlooked or undervalued. The prevailing attitude is that everyone knows what must be done, so why go to lengths to reward it? Stewart, however, takes pains to demonstrate the opposite: to leave a note or a voicemail, or to tell someone in person how much his efforts make a difference. "That's just my style, and it's from the heart," Stewart said. "If it wasn't from the heart, people would recognize it's insincere and not genuine."

Learning from Others' Mistakes

Whether they are advisors, board members, or seasoned colleagues, the people surrounding an entrepreneur have varied and in-depth experiences. In fact, business builders typically seek to attract these individuals in order to tap their knowledge and wisdom, as well as their network of contacts.

Equally important is learning from the mistakes made by

these people who are, no doubt, highly accomplished and competent in their fields. Stewart told of a time the company was entering new markets and she asked a board member who worked in a related industry, "Teach me from your mistakes. It's all about learning. It may not be perfect today, but while it is fresh in your mind, tell me about your story."

In addition to the lessons Stewart learned from their conversation, there was another important takeaway: the need for both parties to put egos aside. As the CEO, she needed the humility, as well as the confidence, to ask for advice and guidance. The director, on the other hand, needed to admit the challenges faced and the mistakes made in order to share the kind of learning that can only come through hard knocks. "People who are unwilling to do that, who always have the answer, who don't want to listen to anybody else, inevitably fail," she added.

Stewart served up a cautionary tale from something she witnessed in the restaurant industry: a leader who rarely sought the counsel of others and who was so unapproachable that people were reluctant to "tell the emperor that he had no clothes," because this executive thought he had all the answers. "Over time, people stopped giving him advice and just went about their business and waited for him to fail, which eventually happened."

Within an established organization, the fate of a leader who doesn't listen may very well be losing her job. For an entrepreneur/founder of a start-up, the outcome may be losing the business. Either way, it is tragic—and often preventable. Leaders need the maturity and native intelligence to listen, ask questions, learn, and do some things differently. The ones who don't do that suffer the consequences of curbing their success.

"I can only speak for DineEquity, but at our company, if you are not willing to listen, if you are not willing to change, if you are not willing to reach across the aisle, then you are not going to be successful here," Stewart added. "Not everybody agrees with this, by the way, but I think the CEO sets the tone because, as my father used to say, 'Fish start stinking at the head.' I really believe that if the CEO doesn't set the standard, ultimately the organization won't be as successful as it can be."

Concurrent with learning from the mistakes of others is listening to their ideas and suggestions. Within a franchise organization such as a restaurant chain, innovations can come from any source, including owners and their employees. The wise leader sees this input as a rich vein to be tapped and evaluated.

"We have entrepreneurs who, every day, want you to listen to them because they think they know how to make an omelet better than we do," Stewart said. "And guess what? They have some really good ideas." She offered the example of one franchisee, who suggested a new approach on bank financing. Her response? "Let's hear what you have to say. Teach me and educate me on your point of view," she added. "And that is the only way that we get better."

Taking on the Big Challenges

Ultimately, leadership is tested in the challenges that arise in the normal course of business or because of a significant step that a company decides to make. Here, there is the potential to leapfrog ahead in terms of growth or new opportunities, but this step is not without its share of challenges. To improve one's chances of success, the entrepreneur must do the necessary groundwork and due diligence, gather input widely—especially from advisors and directors who may have had similar experiences—and then commit to a plan.

For Stewart, the challenge came with the acquisition of Applebee's in 2007, which at the time was a troubled restaurant chain that was larger than IHOP. "I would have to say that it was my greatest personal success because it was against a lot of odds," Stewart recalled. "Six months after the acquisition, there was a global financial crisis. . . . In retrospect, everybody was looking at me and saying, 'Would she fold? Would she crack? Would she fall apart? Would she leave or what would she do?'"

What Stewart did was get up every day and do the necessary work to accomplish the task, with a great deal of courage and tenacity. Failure never entered her mind because she knew what success looked like. Having run Applebee's before, she knew it was a great company in need of a turnaround, not unlike the one she had orchestrated at IHOP. When the *New York Times* interviewed her a month after the deal was announced—following eighteen consecutive quarters of growth at IHOP—Stewart was asked to consider the possibility of having "bet wrong on Applebee's." She dismissed the notion, not out of hubris, but because of the facts at hand. "I don't see it that way," Stewart told the *Times*. "I see it as we successfully turned IHOP into this fabulous successful brand, as measured by top-line sales and franchisee health and consumers—and we are now doing the same exact thing at Applebee's."[2]

Looking back, Stewart spoke with pride for the Applebee's acquisition and integration as an organizational win, which included selling five hundred company-owned restaurants to become a largely franchised business. To execute that strategy, she needed to deliver the message to a room full of general managers, who could have felt that the company was abandoning them. If those general managers chose to leave, it could have hampered the company's success in selling those restaurants; without buyers, the strategy would have failed. In her message to the managers, she emphasized the key takeaway: the brand was all that mattered, not the ownership structure. In the end, most people stayed because of the brand.

In the victory of the Applebee's turnaround, in the midst of a brutally difficult economic environment, is the fruit of the lessons learned by teaching, coaching, and mentoring others. "I feel very good about turning it around [by] sharing the vision and strategy, getting people aligned, socializing [the plan] to anybody who would listen," Stewart recalled. "People wanted to believe."

TIPS FROM THE TITANS

- ☞ Become a teacher, coach, and mentor—even as an entrepreneur who is busy building a business and executing a plan.
- ☞ Realize that you can't scale a business if you are the only one who has the knowledge and expertise. Success comes through others.
- ☞ Make it safe for people to try and fail, and to learn from their mistakes by owning what went wrong—as well as what went right.
- ☞ Learn from the failures of others; surround yourself with people who will share from the experiences of their hard knocks.
- ☞ Don't be afraid of the big challenges that arise, particularly those opportunities to grow and expand.

Chapter Six

Create Value out of a Vision

> *To build a successful business, you've got to have a vision of what you think that business is and what it could become, and how to translate that vision into something operational and meaningful to your employees, customers, and other stakeholders.*
>
> —Robert L. Johnson, Founder, Former Chairman, and CEO, Black Entertainment Television

All entrepreneurs have ideas, but not all of those ideas translate into value. The differentiator is vision. The gestation from idea to vision requires several elements to be brought together, crystallizing what may be largely in an entrepreneur's brain into a tangible and executable plan. Vision moves beyond the initial idea of what an entrepreneur believes and adds the necessary acceptance of the marketplace. From concept to execution and delivery, a business only succeeds if the audience responds: the customer is the deciding factor. To validate a vision, customers must become emotionally engaged with products, services, or solutions for which there is a need or that can positively impact the marketplace.

Through this process, an entrepreneur demonstrates that most elusive of abilities: creating value. Value creation is the ultimate goal for any entrepreneurial venture; without it, there is no sustainability for a business and no track record of success on which to build. The proven ability to create value is key to attracting capital with which to build or expand a business, taking it to the next level.

Robert L. Johnson, founder, former chairman, and CEO of Black Entertainment Television (BET), understands value creation from both sides of the equation. As an entrepreneur he has demonstrated value creation in his businesses, attracting investment capital eager to partner with him. And as an investor he has deployed his own capital in value-generating enterprises, from hotels and investment funds to a National Basketball Association (NBA) franchise. The common theme behind these diverse ventures is a vision that translates into value creation by serving the needs of customers.

"It always starts with a vision of something you believe is needed or that can impact a marketplace or affect a customer base or other stakeholders," Johnson explained. "The thing is...you've got to ask, 'What elements do I need to put it all together?'"

Johnson views his entrepreneurial journey through the lens of being African–American and a minority business leader. "I would say my greatest leadership success is understanding the overall psychology of what it takes for an African–American businessperson in the United States to be successful," he added. "If someone asked, 'What's the secret sauce?' that's it."

At BET, Johnson demonstrated the power of emotional engagement to reach an important population segment: the African–American community. The Museum of Broadcast

Communication credited BET as being "the first and only television network in the United States primarily devoted to the attraction of African–American viewers." With appealing cable television programming, Johnson attracted an audience that advertisers wanted to reach: middle-income African–Americans. This unique and sustainable value proposition eventually led to an explosion in BET's reach through cable technology to key markets nationwide. After he sold BET to Viacom for $3 billion in 2000, Johnson reached a rare pinnacle among titans: becoming a billionaire on the *Forbes* list—the first African-American to do so.

His accomplishments become even more impressive considering where he started: one of ten children of factory-worker parents who valued education but did not serve as role models for entrepreneurship. There was no family business for Johnson to join or take over one day. What he inherited from his parents, however, was even more important: the value of hard work—a trait he shares with all successful entrepreneurs. For a business builder in any field, there is no such thing as "dirty work"—only a job that needs to get done. Over the course of his career, Johnson proved his ability to do what it takes to be successful. In that, he serves as a role model for others who have ideas and visions to turn into plans and actions.

Self-Made Man

The only job that Johnson did not like, and the one he ultimately failed at, was his first: a paper route to deliver the *Rockford Morning Star* in his Illinois town. "I just couldn't get up early enough and face the cold Illinois winters," Johnson laughed. "And so that was the one job I sort of walked out on." His mother's solution was to have his older brother do the morning delivery while Johnson did the collections after school. Over the years, Johnson had plenty of jobs; at the county and state fairs he cleaned bathrooms and worked the grounds. He mowed lawns and did basic landscaping. By the time he was in college, he took factory jobs during the summer. "I was always very comfortable with the fact that you have to work to achieve something, and do the work as long as it was legal or worth doing," he added. "There was no concern that [a job] was dirty work or beneath me. And if I worked at something—other than the paper route—I did my best to make it a successful experience for me and for the person I was working for."

Among wannabe entrepreneurs there can be a disdain for work that gets one's hands dirty, literally or figuratively. Often, it is not the work itself that is onerous, but the concern about others' perceptions. They fear that if they stoop to do a menial job, they will be perceived as inferior by others. True entrepreneurs couldn't care less. All that matters is the urgency of the job and the quality of the work. They do not waste time wondering what others will think of them. Their self-confidence enables them to do whatever it takes to get the job done. Among the most successful entrepreneurs, there is little or no insecurity about who they are; they are secure by nature. The only thing they have to prove is the validity of their ideas, not their sense of self.

"Entrepreneurs are different from people who grew up in corporate America," Johnson observed. "Entrepreneurs are willing to do anything and everything."

There is a strong correlation between being self-possessed and able to take on any job. This entrepreneurial humility is not only productive, it helps keep one's ego in check, which is hugely important for recruiting and retaining the top talent. "Good, talented people or strategic companies don't like dealing with a person [with a big ego]. A company could have great products, but nobody wants to deal with them. So slowly it just erodes," Johnson said. "After a while, your product quality starts to suffer because you're not getting the best people, or some people who could have been beneficial to you go other places and take their intellectual insight and abilities somewhere else."

Another aspect of being a self-made businessperson is the ability to motivate one's self. Johnson spoke with pride as he shared his story of generating possibilities and taking advantage of opportunities. During his youth, the civil rights movement made strides that allowed more minorities to attend college and state institutions of higher learning, which, in turn, encouraged more minority students to stay in high school and graduate.

As a high school senior in Freeport, Illinois, Johnson was one of two African–American students in an advanced English class of about twenty-five. (He was born in Hickory, Mississippi, but spent much of his childhood in Freeport.) One day the teacher asked how many of the students planned to go to college. When all the other students raised their hands, Johnson did too, not wanting to be left out. But he knew his family had no money to send him to college. In fact, he hadn't thought much about continuing his education until the teacher asked the question. His plan at that point was to join the U.S. Air Force and become a fighter pilot.

A month or two later, the teacher asked the class again: of those who said they were going to college, how many had seen a guidance counselor to discuss how to apply and enroll. This time, about 65 percent of students in the class raised their hands, as did Johnson. Now he was convinced: he had to apply. A friend of his was college bound on a football scholarship to the University of Illinois (and later played in the National Football League), which encouraged Johnson also to apply to the University of Illinois. In the end, he was accepted to the university and financed his education with student loans. (In addition to a bachelor's degree from the University of Illinois, he later earned a master's degree in international affairs from the Woodrow Wilson School of Public and International Affairs at Princeton University.)

Johnson's willingness to take a chance and envision a different future for himself fed his entrepreneurial spirit. The same can be said for most entrepreneurs: whether they are born into a family business or create a vision (and themselves) from scratch, they see—and seize—opportunities where others may not. Whether someone comes from wealth or a modest background is not a significant influence; what matters most is one's makeup—her entrepreneurial DNA. Entrepreneurs, particularly those who become titans, are simply wired to find opportunities and realize a vision.

Another common trait among entrepreneurs is self-motivation. These individuals typically don't need a lot of influencers to achieve their goals and attain at least some level of success. They may have role models and champions along the way, but the biggest source of drive and ambition is within.

Achieving the Vision with the Right People

The vision cannot be limited to the entrepreneur, however. As plans take shape, a business builder needs to inspire and engage others. "You've got to have people with the ability to execute on the vision and utilize and deploy capital appropriately," Johnson said. "As the leader or the business manager—the visionary—you've got to make sure you can motivate people to achieve exactly what you conceived as the vision. You've got to make sure you're getting the best people and nurturing them in a way that brings out the best in them."

As the entrepreneurs interviewed and those with whom I've worked can attest, successful execution is ultimately about having the right people. Money, alone, will not be sufficient to achieve the necessary commitment and buy-in to take a business, particularly a start-up, to the next level. A shared vision is needed, from which culture is built. "Once you've got that, it's easy to sustain. Then you're not building ships in the desert. You should have a viable business," Johnson said. "The question now becomes, how big can it be?"

Central to building an effective team is having strong communication skills to share information and empower others. Johnson attributed the foundation of this skill to growing up in a large family, which necessitated a high degree of interaction. Later, he espoused the belief that communication helps to engender trust and confidence in a shared mission. Discussions become more robust as opinions and viewpoints are shared in an environment that encourages give and take.

For entrepreneurs, this type of communication can be a challenge; as the ones with the vision, they are often more comfortable with telling others what to do instead of building consensus. Johnson has described the early stage of an entrepreneurial firm as a "tribe...like hunters and gatherers." With no formal structure other than a "chief," the start-up organization revolves around the work to be done, which is directed from the top. "And as long as people believe in the chief they're O.K., they'll stay around, but there is always infighting," Johnson told the *New York Times* in a November 2011 interview. "And what you tend to do in that situation is to have this kind of primitive reaction—you try to force people to your will. And because you're afraid that people may not do what you want them to do, sometimes you do it for them. And they never get a chance to grow because you're basically telling everybody what to do, when to do it, how to do it."[1]

Johnson admitted this was the dynamic early on at BET, where he tried to do everything and others had to do things his way. "You don't let that control go away until you begin to see the business take shape and get a bit of lift to it," he added. "And then you feel a little more comfortable giving people the authority and the responsibility to do things their way—which was different from the entrepreneurial way, and my way."[2]

Over time, he added, the culture changed into one in which others were empowered to take charge and be more accountable. Then, he could step back and delegate more, ultimately building the skill set and the confidence of his team.

Making an Emotional Connection with Customers

Looking back on the early days of BET, Johnson said he was "not really doing anything new in terms of core business objectives," which amounted to bringing content tailored to the African–American audience, which had been done previously with magazines. Using cable television and satellite technology, however, was a new approach that allowed BET to attract a viewership and tap the growing buying power of the African–American middle class. "With cable and satellite you can target each market with broadcasting with broad appeal," Johnson explained. "And because of the technology, you could aggregate nationally as opposed to just in one market such as Chicago. As an African–American businessman, I saw there was an underserved market that could be served. This [approach] also benefited cable operators who were seeking African–American subscribers to their cable systems, as well as advertisers who wanted to reach African–Americans the same way they could with *Ebony, Essence,* or some other magazines."

Johnson established a powerful emotional connection within his marketplace, anchored in the desires of a community to see images that projected them in a positive light. According to the Museum of Broadcast Communications, the "heart and soul" of BET programming from the beginning was music video, predating MTV by a year and offering a black-oriented music video service. "Indeed, the network's flagship program, *Video Soul,* became a household word in many black communities," it added. As BET grew, programs diversified to include national affairs, interviews, stage presentations, talk shows, jazz, and sports programming from historically black colleges.[3]

Although clearly a pioneer in cable television, Johnson, who was inducted into the *Broadcasting & Cable* magazine's Hall of Fame in 1997, largely shrugged it off with an observation that he "just happened to be at the right place at the right time with the right people."

While working with the National Cable Television Association, an industry trade group, he saw cable being targeted for urban markets and compared this to what had happened with black print media and black radio. "I said, 'Why not this?' And that's essentially how it started," Johnson said. "At that time, I had the vision to see how this technology applied to an old concept of serving a target market that was hungry for content appealing to their interests—and that led to the creation of Black Entertainment Television."

In any venture's success there are elements of timing and even luck, but they only go so far. It takes true talent to build a business, identify and manage risks, and navigate the obstacles, including challenges that are completely outside the entrepreneur's control, such as regulatory changes, a new competitor, or macroeconomic developments. Avoidable in most cases are incidents of what Johnson called "pilot error," mistakes made by the pilot (in this case, the business leader) that causes the aircraft (organization) to falter, fail, or even crash.

"You pull the wrong lever. You want the flaps to go down and, instead, they go up, and it changes the aerodynamics of the plane," Johnson said. "In a business, the same thing can happen.... You simply make the wrong decision and your competition leaps ahead of you. You're no longer relevant to the marketplace.... Bad decisions can make a business fail."

Entrepreneurs who have built and sustained businesses successfully are those who seem to avoid pilot errors more often than those who ultimately fail. One way to avoid errors is to stay closely attuned to the desires of the marketplace in order to deliver exactly what the customer wants. "The companies I build always start out with a vision of what they can be and what they can provide, and then I go after it with that same vision in mind," Johnson explained.

DEALING WITH RISK AND PILOT ERROR

The biggest fear for any company is the unforeseen event and its impact on the decisions that have been made, particularly with regard to enterprise risk. A company normally doesn't run into trouble or fail because it has executed well; instead, it has executed very poorly, which usually stems from having a bad plan. As firms look to select, groom, and develop executives, the ability to identify and deal with risk is a highly desirable talent.

Risk is generally viewed through two lenses. One is financial, guarding against taking on too much debt or not retaining sufficient capital and liquidity. The other is operational—in other words, delegating too much authority without the proper checks and balances. Risk management involves greater diligence to identify potential risks, determine how the company could be impacted, and putting early warning systems in place.

Specifically, companies are looking at major transactions more carefully, with increased focus on the downside. Although the upside potential remains important, leaders and their advisors/board members are more diligent than ever in considering what can go wrong, particularly when leverage is involved. In addition, every strategy comes with execution risk, and when an acquisition is made there is always integration risk.

Risk management is an ongoing discipline that involves every facet of a company's strategy and execution. Robust discussions must take place about the appropriate amount of risk to be taken in the current environment.

Value Creation

Ultimately, the viability of any business is judged by its ability to create value. Although this is a critical distinction for any entrepreneur, from Johnson's perspective it is even more important for minority business owners who, he believes, have not always had the same access to capital as other groups.

Demographics aside, value creation is the key that unlocks capital sources. Financiers and private investors tend to look at new ventures with a jaundiced eye until there is a track record that shows revenue generation, profitability, and sustainability. When an entrepreneur distinguishes himself with the ability to create value out of a vision, his success becomes part of his personal brand. As Johnson observed, "The brand means that you can pick up your phone and call people. Then they accept you...as a value guy. You can drive value."

Johnson candidly shared examples in which he was approached partly because he was an African–American businessman and the federal government had mandated minority participation in a project. But ethnicity is not what ultimately made him the go-to person; successful value creation was.

"If you want to build businesses of scale, then first and foremost you've got to demonstrate that you are a value driver, that you can create wealth. I can't stress that enough," Johnson added. "If you can't, by your work ethic and your behavior, demonstrate the ability to create confidence—so that the dominant power structure in the free-market economy that we have here can embrace you—it's going to be extremely difficult to achieve scale, unless you are some unique talent so that it really doesn't matter. But most people aren't Michael Jackson, Oprah Winfrey, or Tiger Woods."

94

The entrepreneur who wants and needs to access capital must acknowledge the way the system works: attracting investors' attention and garnering their support the first time can be extremely difficult, but after one or more successes it becomes much easier. By the time someone reaches the titan stage, having created a large, sustainable business network or a series of start-ups, investors will be far more likely to entertain a proposal. Knowing an entrepreneur's track record, they might even seek out a chance to be part of the next venture.

"While there is plenty of capital, if you can't get it, it doesn't matter how much is there; you simply can't get it," Johnson said. "And if you can't get strategic partners to help you grow and navigate in a particular sector, you run the risk of being overtaken by somebody who has the assets—both the capital and the strategic relations. That's the message I give to people...and it is particularly important for minority businesses."

When the Entrepreneur Becomes an Investor

In the later stages of his entrepreneurial career, Johnson went from being an operator to a supplier of capital. His ventures post-BET include: launching a $2.5 billion private equity real estate fund and taking it public on the New York Stock Exchange; partnering with the Carlyle Group in a $250 million private equity fund; partnering with Mack McLarty, former chief of staff to President Bill Clinton, in establishing a billion-dollar automobile dealership group, and raising $150 million to acquire two media companies. Johnson, who in media interviews has called such investment ventures "my second act," exemplifies the maturation of an entrepreneur from the one trying to attract others to his vision to being the holder of capital who wants to invest in others' ventures.

Although each role is distinct—the entrepreneur/operator and the entrepreneur/investor—there is important commonality between them. In both capacities, the focus is on the scope and depth of the vision. What will ultimately decide its validity is the likelihood that it will achieve the primary target: creating value.

TIPS FROM THE TITANS

- ☛ Establish a track record for creating value, which is the key to attracting capital to build or expand a business.
- ☛ Identify the elements you must bring together to impact the marketplace, make a positive impact on customers, and meet the needs of other stakeholders.
- ☛ Embrace "entrepreneurial humility" to do whatever work needs to be done to reach a goal, make a difference—and keep one's ego in check.
- ☛ Commit to strong communication to build a team and inform and empower others.
- ☛ Make an emotional connection with the marketplace by being closely attuned to the desires of the marketplace.

Chapter Seven

Be True to Yourself

I'm chairman of everything and CEO of nothing.

I focus on the areas where I have expertise.

—Sam Zell, Chairman, Equity Group Investments

There are two basic varieties of entrepreneurs in the business world. The first is the business builder/operator. Hands on and deeply involved, these leaders possess the proven abilities to conceive of a plan and bring it to reality. The second type of entrepreneur is the incubator. From a thirty-thousand-foot view, and sometimes looking across several industries, the entrepreneur/incubator sees potential based on macroeconomic trends, and then dives closer to the landscape to examine specific business opportunities. The incubator, however, most likely will not run the business; in fact, he typically considers it a strategic advantage to find the best talent to take charge of the operations. That, in the proverbial nutshell, is Sam Zell, entrepreneur and incubator of businesses.

"I'm chairman of everything and CEO of nothing," quipped Zell, who serves as chairman of Equity Group Investments, which he founded more than forty years ago, as well as chairman of five public companies. "I am involved in strategy and direction, in bringing opportunities to our companies through my network, and in major problem-solving. I don't run business operations." Admittedly, Zell's path is not for every entrepreneur; in fact, most will be operators, although a few (as in the case of Robert Johnson, founder of BET) will transition from hands-on business builder to an incubator and provider of capital. Whatever the pathway and the involvement, the important lesson here is to know yourself, to play to your strengths—whether you go out and raise capital to start your own business or you eventually become a Sam Zell, seeking different opportunities in which to invest. Zell's story, and that of every leader profiled in this book, shows that there is more than one way to become a titan. Many paths lead to the pinnacle. The challenge for the business builder is to find the one that is the most authentic given her strengths, natural talent, and vision.

For Zell, what makes the most sense is taking what he calls an owner's approach; that is, focusing on the big picture side of things. "I'm very comfortable delegating day-to-day operations," he said. However, this should not be mistaken for disinterest. He is highly involved in strategic decisions—the "major stuff," as he called it, such as the financing, acquisition, and disposition of businesses. With a clear demarcation between his role as chairman and that of his operating executives, he extends his reach as a serial entrepreneur. (Zell also believes that the chairman and CEO roles ought to be separated in large, publicly traded companies, as advocated by many shareholder groups, to improve governance.)

The Rope Theory

The separation of duties, Zell believes, allows real talent to shine as individuals are given even more responsibility to act independently. He calls it his "rope theory"—he gives people enough latitude to either prove themselves or fail. The rope, as he explained, can be used as a lasso, corralling like-minded, performance-driven individuals in support of a plan and in alignment with overarching corporate goals. The alternative, in irreverent Zell-speak, is that "they can hang themselves."

Zell's unabashed straight talk points to a fundamental truth for every entrepreneur who needs to build a team: it's all about execution. To be successful, companies need the right people for the job, those who can pull together a team, absorb the guidance from the chairman and other advisors, and exercise the necessary discipline to operate a company toward sustainable success. For the entrepreneur, finding the right fit is crucial, balancing the "big picture" focus and idea-generation of the chairman/advisor with the execution strengths of the on-the-ground executives. This is an important takeaway for any entrepreneur, whether he has one business or a portfolio of enterprises, like Zell. As observed previously, at some point the business builder cannot go it alone. For someone like Zell, that point is reached immediately; his strategy is to find a business investment opportunity and simultaneously identify or bring in the best talent to run the operations. Similarly, the more traditional business builder/entrepreneur will have to bring in complementary talent with strengths where the founder is weak.

Delegation of responsibilities, but not of risk, is the prerequisite for getting to the next level. Ultimately, entrepreneurs who are unable or unwilling to take this next step, who cannot accept the realities of who they are, will fail in their quest to become titans. Their inability to move beyond themselves as individuals will limit the development of their enterprises because they cannot segue from the hands-on, do-it-all individual to the visionary, strategic business builder/advisor who acts like a chairman while others handle more of the day-to-day operations.

Part and parcel of this leadership dynamic are mutual respect and appreciation for the strengths that each party brings to the partnership. By extension, respect has to be earned from direct reports throughout the organization. This is the key to true leadership, Zell believes. "You are able to lead because people respect you and seek your viewpoints," he said.

At the same time, people at all levels of the organization need to take responsibility for their decisions and actions. Accountability is crucial. For operating executives, this means ensuring that the business is running efficiently, with an eye toward future sustainable growth. "They have to remember that they're responsible," Zell added.

And when it's time to take a bow for a job well done, the true leader readily gives credit to the team. "Strong leaders reward their teams by recognizing their successes," he said. The worst-case scenario is when "a leader unduly steals credit for a success."

For Zell this is a fatal flaw. "Someone who doesn't have people skills ultimately can't be a leader."

Recognizing Opportunity

Zell's prodigious success was presaged at a young age with a knack for recognizing opportunity, a talent that has continued throughout his career with the development of a keen eye. As a twelve-year-old attending Hebrew school in Chicago, he "imported" *Playboy* magazine from the city to resell in the suburbs, where the publication wasn't available. In college, at the University of Michigan, he started a party favor business (the most popular item was a fourteen-foot cloth snake). Such an early appetite for entrepreneurial ventures set his course for life. (Zell noted that, except for four days in a law firm, he has never worked for anyone else.) This raises the question discussed earlier in the book: Are business builders born or made?

In an interview with *Leaders Magazine*, Zell said he believed entrepreneurship can be found in virtually everyone, although this proclivity varies in intensity among individuals. "My objectives in this arena have been to create environments that will help individuals recognize and nurture that element within themselves, as well as identify those very few who are entrepreneurial to their core," he added. "In particular, those in this latter group, who thrive on taking risks and being out on their own, have no traditional road map. I took that route early in my career..."[1]

While at college, Zell teamed up with an entrepreneurial kindred spirit, fraternity brother Robert Lurie, an engineering student at the University of Michigan. Zell had started an apartment management business while he was an undergrad, and hired Lurie to manage one of the buildings. Later, the two of them grew a business empire through Equity Group Investments, based in Chicago, which started in the real estate sector but later branched out with investments in other industries.

Today, Equity Group's investment portfolio includes

interests in real estate, energy, logistics, transportation, media, and health care—most of which are asset-intensive businesses. Companies in which Zell owns a substantial interest and for which he serves as chairman include: Anixter International Inc., a leading global provider of communications, security, and wire and cable products; Equity Lifestyle Properties, Inc., an equity real estate investment trust (REIT) that owns and operates resort and manufactured home communities; Equity Residential, the largest apartment REIT in the United States; Capital Trust, a specialized real estate finance company; and Covanta Holding Corporation, an international owner/operator of energy-from-waste and power generation projects. Previously, he was chairman of Equity Office Properties Trust, which he sold in 2007 to Blackstone Group for $39 billion, the largest private equity deal in history at the time.

From the early days of Equity Group Investments, Zell was the "outside man," concentrating on building business relationships and doing deals. Lurie worked largely behind the scenes, making sure the businesses flowed and minding the finances, while also developing a team of employees. Then, at the age of forty-six, Lurie was diagnosed with advanced colon cancer. Lurie never gave into his illness and instead became a champion and role model for others. Before his death in 1990, Lurie and his wife, Ann, endowed a cancer treatment center at Northwestern University, The Robert H. Lurie Comprehensive Cancer Center. Among the other philanthropic activities championed by the two partners are the Samuel Zell & Robert H. Lurie Institute for Entrepreneurial Studies at the University of Michigan and the Samuel Zell and Robert Lurie Real Estate Center, permanently endowed by Zell in 1998 at The Wharton School of the University of Pennsylvania. (The center was originally established in 1983 to foster excellence in real estate education and research.)

Zell's reflection on his early entrepreneurial days, when there was no "senior person" around to act as the boss or to provide direction (unlike today, when he is the advisor behind the scenes), demonstrated how success came from learning by doing and following the logical path. "You have to be a quick learner. Obviously, our sophistication grew as we learned from everything around us and developed our own ideas." Among the most critical lessons learned, he added, is "recognition of the opportunity."

According to the history of Equity Group Investments, the first opportunities were found amid the massive overbuilding of commercial property in the 1970s that forced developers to abandon properties, which became the makings of a high-quality portfolio of underperforming properties. As the economic recession spread, investments in undervalued but high-quality assets were found in the retail and office markets. In the 1980s, the same approach was applied to other industries by targeting asset-heavy companies with distressed holdings that could be repositioned to generate growth, including rail, container leasing, passenger cruise lines, plastics packaging, agricultural chemicals, and industrial manufacturing. By the 1990s, the portfolio included investments in grocery, radio, bedding, sports equipment, drug stores, and airlines. Later that decade, Zell also expanded to real estate outside the United States through a separate investment firm. Since 2000, Equity Group Investments has also focused on opportunities to take significant ownership stakes, through debt securities, in operations that need restructuring.[2]

Looking for opportunities means focusing on the unique,

whether it's a different approach to the marketplace or a niche business that shows the potential for expansion. Zell cited the example of Homex Development, a home-building company serving middle-class consumers in Mexico. The company captured Zell's attention in the mid-1990s because of what he saw as virtually unlimited demand for low-cost housing in Mexico. "When we got involved with Homex, the company was building a thousand houses a year," Zell said. "What we gave them, in addition to capital, was a partner that provided best practices in scaling operations and in corporate governance. We guided them as they went from a thousand houses a year to eighty-five thousand houses a year."

In the process, Zell and his team brought Homex to the New York Stock Exchange, where it raised ample capital to fuel its growth—and all because of a recognized opportunity to expand. True to his role as an incubator, however, Zell never had anything to do with Homex's day-to-day operations. Instead, he provided the guidance and the direction to enable the company to go public.

With such diverse operations, Zell exhibits another aspect of knowing oneself. While a titan such as Bill Marriott has a name synonymous with hospitality, Zell never felt bound by any one industry. "I think I would be less effective...because I'm much more eclectic," he added. "That doesn't make someone else any less of an entrepreneur or me any less of an entrepreneur. I just enjoy absorbing macro information and applying it to more micro decisions."

By focusing on the "macro," the big picture and the prevailing trends in the economy or in society, Zell searches for emerging patterns and diverse areas to explore, where there are unfulfilled consumer needs or a struggling industry that might yield good companies in need of a turnaround. Once he locks in on potential opportunity, he goes "micro," zooming in to find specific investments. For other entrepreneurs, Zell's approach may be unappealing or impossible. Nonetheless, his perspective yields an important lesson for all business builders: you can never lose sight of the macro picture. Indeed, all the titans profiled in this book—including those who specialize in one industry—are masters of this approach. No matter the business or industry, entrepreneurs must consider the broader economic trends, from the impact of globalization to how technology is changing the business. Keeping one's eyes too close to the micro causes myopia. By understanding the macro and executing (or, in Zell's case, empowering execution) in the micro, an entrepreneur stands a better chance of building a business that can stand the test of time.

Zell reached into his portfolio of stories to share an example, this time of acquiring control of an overleveraged radio company in Cincinnati in 1993. Several years later, federal regulations changed the ownership limit from seventeen stations to an unlimited number of stations but no more than 40 percent market share. Zell told his team to "go out and buy every radio station they could."Lauding his management team that "was capable of meeting the challenge," Zell related how the company went from seventeen stations to two hundred and thirty-two in twenty-four months. "We saw the opportunity, we executed, and we made a fortune." Zell, who started as a "real estate guy," demonstrates that his secret to success is not limited, as they say in the property business, to "location, location, location." Rather, it's all about timing and opportunity, using the macro to identify trends and then shifting to the micro to find specific businesses that have the potential for the big return.

"The Enemy Is Without'

Another tagline of Zell's success—which he calls "Sam-isms"—reminds people exactly where the competition is. "The enemy is without," Zell stated, a favorite Sam-ism that is illustrated by a cartoon of a wagon train drawn into a circle. The concept is that inside, within the team, there is support, protection, and cohesion. Outside the circle are the predators and competitors.

"In the context of leadership, that means there's never an internal door closed to you," Zell added. "Our culture is one of transparency and collaboration. In forty years, I've never closed the door to my office."

He shared the story of a bankrupt telecommunications company bought by his firm in 1985. The company was known to have an impressive art collection, which Zell wanted to view after hours, so he returned to the headquarters over the weekend. As he walked around the building, what struck him more than the pictures on the wall were all the locked doors. "I never forgot that. Here was a failed company—at the time the largest bankruptcy in the United States—and every single office door was locked," he said. "What does this mean? Does one person not trust another person to the point that every night all their stuff is locked up and inaccessible?"

Turf-protecting mentality (as opposed to confidential papers or sensitive documents that need to be locked up for security reasons) is a "derailer" as far as Zell is concerned. In an entrepreneurial environment, closed doors stop the flow of ideas, interrupt the exchange of information, and can even fracture the team. At the head of that team is the entrepreneur who, in an advisory role, should literally have an open door—he needs to be always accessible, whether to counsel, console, or correct.

"Culture relates to what I call people skills," Zell said. "There are times when you have to be [extremely tough]. And then there are times when you have to be the person everyone wants to come to when they've got a problem."

This truth underscores the fact that, for the entrepreneur, it's all about execution. At the end of the day, an operation that doesn't have a team that works well together, is unwilling to self-criticize, and is unable to share ideas, cannot build a successful company. The business builder cannot execute all by himself. Therefore, fostering a team whose members collaborate rather than compete with each other is crucial.

EVALUATING CEO PERFORMANCE

In any organization, evaluation of and accountability for performance must go all the way to the top. The same standards that hold true for large publicly traded companies also apply in general to entrepreneurial ventures in which there is an operating executive in charge of day-to-day activity.

The CEO (or operating executive) evaluation process must be tailored to fit each company. In general, a process that is more formal tends to be have more impact. No matter the form, the process should be highly confidential. (In large companies, the chairman of the board or the chairman of the governance/compensation committee assumes the leadership role in the performance evaluation process.)

(continued)

Once board leadership has been appointed, the CEO evaluates her own performance in the current year against stated goals. This should include goals related to the annual plan and any longer-term strategic plan. Ideally, this process should take place annually and should cover each performance objective for the CEO.

Following the CEO self-assessment, the appointed outside directors should meet independently to discuss it, and then conduct their own evaluations that are conveyed to the designated director for consolidation. The outside directors should then review and approve the evaluation, and the designated director should meet privately with the CEO to discuss the consolidated evaluation. Finally, the CEO should meet with the outside directors to react to the evaluation and discuss appropriate next steps.

Evaluating CEO performance takes time, thoughtful analysis, and candor from directors. However, the benefits are tremendous, especially in strengthening the relationship between the CEO and the board. To be effective, such evaluations require a clear position description, mutually agreed performance measures, and a performance feedback mechanism. Accomplished in this way, CEO evaluations can result in greatly improved CEO performance.

Don't Take Yourself Too Seriously

Zell is known to be bold, candid, and often irreverent. His decades-long track record of restructuring and growing companies is impressive. He has created tens of thousands of jobs. Yet the processes of rebuilding troubled businesses often require unpopular decisions that invite criticism. Zell shrugs it all off with one comment, his "Eleventh Commandment": "Thou shalt not take oneself too seriously."

Entrepreneurs, no matter how experienced or stellar their track records, will still make mistakes. Success does not mean infallibility. Asked about his biggest disappointment, Zell immediately replied, "The Tribune Company," referring to a leveraged buyout in 2007 that gave him control of Tribune Company, which owns the *Los Angeles Times*, *Chicago Tribune*, and other newspapers and television stations. In a quick post-mortem of the deal, Zell noted that he and his team never had the time to execute his plan for the company when the bottom fell out of the market. The leveraged buyout closed just months before the "great recession," and Tribune Company filed for bankruptcy less than a year later. Zell committed about $315 million of his own money in the deal.

While counter to his original plan for the company, Zell and his team were forced to make dramatic cost cuts. "We had to take a billion dollars out of the costs," Zell said. In the process, Zell was pilloried in the press. "Somebody once said the media loves covering nothing more than the media," he said. "That is an understatement."

The deal created "way too much exposure," he added. "For the first twenty years of my career, I did very well under a rock," referring to his preference to limit time in the limelight.

A titan the likes of Sam Zell has hardly ever existed "under a rock." He has found opportunities in a variety of industries and realized tremendous success in the vast majority of deals. Success for him has meant deviating from the "herd," going against the prevailing trend and the conventional wisdom that, in time, will most likely be proven wrong. When the herd is thundering ahead, such as in a real estate sector that is showing signs of overbuilding, Zell knows the real opportunities are to be found by blazing a trail in another direction toward opportunities that others cannot yet see.

"It starts with an inordinate amount of self-confidence, which enables you to stick to your decision despite conventional wisdom or what others may or may not be doing," Zell told *Leaders Magazine*. "In addition, real entrepreneurs have an innate tendency to not just recognize problems, but to see solutions. These two truths have repeatedly intersected throughout my career."[3]

That's not to say that Zell hasn't had his share of challenges along the way, but his commitment has always been to find solutions that translate into opportunity. This, perhaps, is the real secret to his success and the underlying belief that has taken a talent for entrepreneurship displayed at a young age into a multi-industry business empire: Zell knows himself and what he's good at. By sticking with that, he's become a titan.

TIPS FROM THE TITANS

- ☛ Know yourself and your strengths. For example, are you an operator by nature or do you see yourself as an incubator who will partner with others to execute the plan day to day?
- ☛ Success comes from delegating to others and developing a bench of talent. An entrepreneur cannot be a one-person army.
- ☛ Mutual respect and trust are paramount. A team that competes within will not survive.
- ☛ Even if you have a narrow focus, never lose sight of the macroeconomic view, particularly the outside factors that will impact the business.
- ☛ Empower and encourage entrepreneurial thinking and actions in others on your team by providing opportunities to grow, develop, and acquire new skills and experiences.

Chapter Eight

Take a Risk to Do Things Differently

You have to be willing to look at things a little bit differently, and be okay with the possibility that you might fail."

—Richard "Rick" Federico, Chairman and CEO, P.F. Chang's China Bistro, Inc.

To be an entrepreneur is to blaze your own trail, heading in an entirely new direction or, at least, taking a different approach to fulfilling consumers' needs and exceeding their expectations. Innovation is a prerequisite, but truly only table stakes for getting into the game. Those who succeed in building businesses, who take a concept to reality and then to a sustainable enterprise, are those who can look at things through a different lens and are willing to try the new and different, even though there is the possibility (but hopefully not the probability) of failure.

Richard "Rick" Federico, chairman and CEO of P.F. Chang's China Bistro, Inc., had a role model early in life for calculated risk taking: his father, who, after meeting a young woman from Illinois while she was traveling in Italy, married her and later moved to the United States. Although he did not speak much English and had never been outside of Italy, he did not hesitate to start a new life, with jobs that ranged from a one-time gig of modeling golf wear to working as a community developer in Arizona, literally giving sales pitches to potential customers from the side of the road, and eventually becoming international sales director for the development firm.

After moving to the Chicago area, Federico's father designed and developed a high-end Italian restaurant, which suddenly became the family business. Watching his father in action, Federico came to appreciate his "straightforward, no B.S. kind of personality that people gravitated to," and his perspective on life that things are not "half full or half empty, but 90 percent full, 100 percent of the time." As Federico observed, "I think that perspective, versus being a little more cynical and assuming the negative side to every circumstance, has helped me in my career."

From the family restaurant to stints with the major chains—including Steak and Ale, Grady's Good Times, and P.F. Chang's—Federico has exhibited much of the same optimism as his father, being willing to see opportunities where others see only obstacles, or as he put it, "betting on yourself." At P.F. Chang's, Federico was willing to develop multiple Asian restaurants even though others had tried and failed. Moreover, he went up against the fundamental belief that one needed to be Asian to do Asian cuisine (although plenty of good Italian restaurants had debunked the myth of needing "mama in the kitchen" to be successful).

In honor of his success as a business builder, Federico was named the 2012 winner of the Norman Award from *Nation's Restaurant News*, recognizing his leadership in fostering the growth and development of P.F. Chang's. Federico has held the CEO title at P.F. Chang's since 1997 and served as chairman since 1998. Under his leadership, the chain has grown to more than two hundred restaurants in thirty-nine states. A second concept, Pei Wei Asian Diner, was launched in 2000 and now has 173 units in twenty-three states.

The Norman Award is named for the late Norman Brinker, chairman emeritus and former CEO of Brinker International, one of the world's leading casual-dining restaurant organizations. Brinker was also one of Federico's mentors in the business. Excluding his mother and father, Federico considers Brinker to have been one of the most important influences in his life. "The best ever was Norman Brinker, by far," Federico said, when asked about notable titans in the restaurant business. "He was iconic because what Norman did very successfully was surround himself with really good people. You can go back and track the numbers of restaurant industry leaders from a variety of companies that all connect back to Norman and having worked for Norman. He was really good at taking talent and letting them run their businesses. So you would collaborate with Norman, you would work with Norman, but at the end of the day, you were accountable for executing a strategic plan and an operational plan, while Norman was always there as a support."

A second influencer was Bill Regas, a well-regarded restaurateur and owner of the longest-running restaurant in Tennessee, who later supported the development of Grady's Goodtimes, a casual concept that Federico helped to launch at one point in his career. "I affectionately call Bill the 'chairman.' He was the guy who, when we started the Grady's concept, was the mentor... who glued everybody together," Federico added. "What I love about Bill is he is intensely competitive, but he is also the most positive leader that you would ever want to be around.... He understands the importance of maintaining a close personal relationship with people he works with. He does it in a way that you never, ever want to disappoint the 'chairman.' "

Long before going to work for Brinker and Regas, however, Federico worked with his first role model and mentor: his father.

Learning the Restaurant Business

After graduating from the University of Tennessee, Federico's original plan was to go to law school. About that time, his father had bought his Italian restaurant and hired an executive chef and a manager. Because Federico had worked at Steak and Ale Restaurants during college, along with his roommate, it seemed logical that they would spend the summer after college graduation working for Federico's father, bartending and waiting tables. Halfway through the summer, his father's manager quit and moved to Canada. That was the day Federico and his friend became managers.

"Knowing what I know today, I would have fired me immediately," Federico laughed, displaying a trait that, while perhaps not directly attributable to long-term success, was certainly common enough among the titans interviewed for this book: most looked back on their early years with a combination of humility, good humor, and fondness.

The restaurant ranged from "modestly successful to a modest failure, depending on any given month." When his father entertained the idea of selling the restaurant, Federico decided to take a few days off to watch a basketball tournament in Atlanta between the University of Tennessee and UCLA. While there, he bumped into a close college friend and fraternity brother, Mike Connor, who worked for Steak and Ale as a general manager in Knoxville, Tennessee. One thing led to another and, after an interview, Federico entered the manager training program and worked for Connor in Knoxville. Federico and his wife, Peggy, were married shortly thereafter, and as his career advanced, the couple moved eleven times in the first nine years of their marriage.

One day Federico's boss approached him with a proposition. He could go to Memphis, Tennessee, to run a restaurant, or he could sign on with the company's newest venture: rebranding underperforming Steak and Ales that were being converted to Orville Bean's Flying Machine and Fix-It Shops, designed to be fun and casual pub-style eateries. The concept was not without risk, as there were only two units in operation. The upside was that if it worked, Federico could showcase his talent and advance his career. Being no stranger to taking calculated risks and being willing to do something new and different, Federico went with Orville Bean's. The result was some success, although conversion costs and other economic factors made the company decide, ultimately, to keep these units as Steak and Ales.

Next stop on Federico's career path was assisting the company in its launch of Bennigan's, which in time would be one of the fastest-growing casual dining chains in America. Then, opportunity knocked again to partner with former colleague Mike Connor and the Regas family in Knoxville to develop the Grady's concept, aimed at the upper end of casual dining. Over the next six years, Grady's became a regional chain, with units in North Carolina, Georgia, Alabama, and Tennessee.

When Grady's was acquired by Norman Brinker in 1989, Federico became part of the Chili's restaurant chain, which he called "my opportunity to get an MBA in restaurant development without going to business school." At the time, the

Chili's organization was in talks to acquire Romano's Macaroni Grill from founder Phil Romano. Given his ethnicity and his background in his father's restaurant, Federico was the ideal candidate to become the head of development for Macaroni Grill. Once again, a risk, but one that Federico gladly took on because of the opportunity to expand his skill set and portfolio of experiences. Thus, from 1988 to 1996 he was president and head of the Italian division for Brinker International. (As more restaurant concepts were added, the name of the parent company was changed from Chili's to Brinker International.)

Working closely with Norman Brinker, Federico developed the first eighty-five Macaroni Grill restaurants, which he considers a formative experience. Opportunity, however, was about to knock again. While vacationing in Arizona, Federico and his wife, at the recommendation of the hotel concierge, visited a Chinese restaurant. Over drinks and then dinner, they took in the design and the décor, the music, the wine list—in short the entire dining experience. Listening to his wife's reaction, Federico realized this restaurant had high consumer appeal. The name of the place was P.F. Chang's.

A few days later, he received a phone call out of the blue from a recruiter about an opportunity to lead brand expansion for an upper-end casual dining restaurant chain, which had attracted venture capital interest. "I'm working for the best company in America," Federico told the recruiter. "I'm working with Norman Brinker, who is iconic in our industry. I love my job, my compensation is great, I love where I live, and my kids are happy." In short, there was no incentive for Federico to look at any other restaurant company, except for one condition: "Unless it is P.F. Chang's," he added. Flabbergasted, the recruiter responded: "How did you know?"

As Federico shared his story, it was clear that luck or perhaps serendipity played a role at certain points in his career. Indeed, many successful entrepreneurs, including those profiled in this book, seem to have the knack for being at the proverbial right place at the right time in order to make and capitalize upon fortuitous connections. What may actually be occurring, however, is the innate ability of the entrepreneur to make the most of those connections. Having found their career paths, often at an early point in their lives, they have a single-mindedness that drives their success forward. For any entrepreneur, what's needed is the right kind of instincts that are then enhanced by learning lessons as he matures, makes mistakes, and achieves success. The differentiator between those who try and those who succeed may very well be the ability to attract mentors and make the most of every experience along the way. Those who devote themselves to continuous development and build the depth and breadth of their understanding will ultimately take their organizations and themselves to a higher level.

Thus, for Federico, the P.F. Chang opportunity did not just parachute out of the sky (although his dining experience there seemed to have an element of kismet to it). Rather, as a successful restaurant executive, he would naturally be high on anyone's list of people to recruit for a chain expansion. And, given his experience in the industry, it makes perfect sense that he would view a new dining concept with a discerning eye. For Federico and P.F. Chang's, the fit seemed made to order.

An Asian Concept Goes National

Founded in 1993 in Scottsdale, Arizona, by Paul Fleming and Philip Chiang (the restaurant name was simplified to Chang), the concept had an impressive pedigree: Philip's mother, Celia Chiang, had founded the Mandarin Restaurant in San Francisco, and Philip had owned the Mandarin Restaurant in Beverly Hills. As he examined the opportunity from all sides, Federico concluded that "if someone could figure this out, the upside could be really, really interesting. My barometer reading for taking these types of risks was if it blew up on me and it didn't work, I could go back—maybe not necessarily to the same company—but I could go back and run something for somebody and be happy doing it." As long as that possibility realistically existed—that taking on this new challenge wouldn't burn any bridges—then the decision was obvious: with the P.F. Chang's concept, the downside was very low and the upside was potentially large, to the point of being virtually limitless.

Federico brought to P.F. Chang's his knowledge and experience in expansion and brand extension, especially what he learned at Chili's and Brinker International—what we might call right-sizing. Taking a rifle-shot approach, leading companies are selective about their openings and discerning about whether a concept has matured at, say, 100 units instead of the original plan of 150. Optimism and enthusiasm must be counterbalanced with a view that too much expansion can turn a positive into a negative. This lesson applies directly to unit-based businesses that are location-driven, such as hotels, restaurants, and retailers, which can face oversaturation. It is a fact of life that not all units will be optimal performers. Opening too many exposes the organization to the risk that new units will cannibalize business from more established ones, or that a secondary location will fail to draw customers.

The broader lesson for entrepreneurs in any business is to avoid overexpansion and over-hiring. Letting your ego get the best of you may lead to the unsubstantiated conclusion that you can keep growing indefinitely. Ultimately, success in business building is about having enough rationality and discipline to know your market and when to stop expanding.

"A brand has a certain size and a certain life cycle," Federico explained. Rather than try to push P.F. Chang's beyond what would be rational for that brand, the company opted also to explore opportunities with other concepts, such as the Pei Wei Asian Diner. "You are not going to be all things to all people," he added.

Another lesson from Federico's lengthy time in the restaurant business comes from observing a well-known company, Darden Restaurants, which owns Olive Garden. After Darden decided to elevate that brand, it invested in more training, sent chefs to culinary school in Italy, upgraded the wine list, made capital investments in the facilities, and launched a successful marketing campaign. The process and the result greatly impressed Federico.

"I have tried to be, as much as possible, a student of other people's successes and failures," Federico said. "I look to companies like Darden that have done a really good job... building a sustainable business. Because there are plenty of examples in our industry of what can be really, really good concepts and good restaurants, but not necessarily the good sort of multi-unit businesses." The Darden/Olive Garden example provides proof positive of the need to keep a business fresh and relevant, and to evolve the brand continuously—a valuable lesson for any business in any industry.

The Emotional Connection of Ownership

Through interviews with thousands of young restaurant managers, Federico came to appreciate that the common desire among most of them is to be an owner. Ownership, however, is more than just equity; it is also a source of pride and personal satisfaction. Tapping into that emotional connection enables a parent company to partner with highly motivated individuals who are eager to think and act like leaders on the local level—doing the hiring, developing and training the team, establishing and monitoring procedures—without shouldering all the risk, because of the resources and support available from the parent company. "At the end of the day, they've got the emotional benefit of walking into the grocery store as the owner of the local P.F. Chang's, and we've got the benefit of getting a highly committed, highly experienced leader in every one of our initial restaurants," Federico said.

The approach has been a win–win, as enthusiastic local partners helped P.F. Chang's break ground as a successful Asian restaurant chain, something that had not been done before, according to Federico. Everywhere he looked, the big companies such as Brinker, Darden, and Outback Steakhouse had multiple brands with casual dining, steakhouse, bar and grill, and Italian themes, but none had Asian. As the first P.F. Chang's units became successful, other interested parties came forward with resources to join the partnership program, which enabled the company to expand to cities such as Miami, Washington DC, Chicago, Dallas, Las Vegas, Houston, and New Orleans.

"The quality and the caliber of the partners we were able to put in the stores...gave us the chance to establish the brand before the big guys could basically step up and say, 'Boy, are we missing an opportunity here!'" Later on, there would be competition; Brinker International, for example, acquired a concept called Big Bowl as an Asian competitor to P.F. Chang's. But by being the first out of the gate, P.F. Chang's was able to gain an edge in several markets and validate its rifle-shot approach to being selective about restaurant locations.

The entrepreneurial takeaway here is to understand the power of ownership, as it impacts what a partner/owner is willing to do to elevate a business versus someone who only has the authority and responsibility to manage the business. "I don't care if it's a restaurant business or a hotel or a retail store, the time, energy, and effort that people generate with that emotional connection of ownership...is significant and clearly applicable," Federico said.

The other side of that coin is failure to empower and engage others on the emotional level; for example, because the owner/founder insists upon calling all the shots or won't entertain the ideas and feedback of others. Without that input, it's easy for a myopic leader to lose focus and discipline and make a serious error, such as picking a real estate location that cannot be supported. In restaurants or any unit-based business, the danger is assuming that the name alone will draw customers anywhere. Or, as Federico said, that today's popularity and success means it's okay to take a "B" location instead of looking for the right "A" location, based on the belief that the customer will go around the corner to find you. "You do that too many times and you wake up one day and you have got a very different organization."

Helping Others Become Successful

When asked to look at his own successes, Federico doesn't go for the obvious, the one that has won him recognition within the industry: the development of P.F. Chang's. He believes, instead, that his more important successes have involved the development of people.

"I like being in restaurants, working on the development of new products and new designs. I like the things that touch the customer and touch the employees," Federico said. To complement his own skill set, he has surrounded himself with people who have the skills and talents that complete the team. "Being able to craft that has, to a large degree, allowed me to really enjoy what I do for a very long period of time," he added.

Federico cited some operating officers who were good and talented people, very intelligent and aggressive, with incredibly high standards. They hired and developed great teams, but were considered "rough around the edges"—they could be abrasive or difficult to get along with at times. In some cases, Federico recalled, his boss would say, "That person has to go." Within reason, Federico will try to smooth out those "rough spots," as he called them, but a cultural mismatch will not be tolerated.

CULTURAL COMPATIBILITY

Within any organization, cultural compatibility is a success factor that outweighs individual talent or the ability of a "superstar" to generate big revenues and profits. This trait may be

(continued)

characterized differently by various organizations, but it comes down to recognizing the importance of the collective good over the benefit to any one individual, no matter how stellar a performer. Put another way: beware the individual who says, "me, me, me," instead of "we, we, we."

This problem can be challenging for organizations, particularly entrepreneurial ones that are so intensely focused on growth and gaining market share. However, it can become tempting to overlook certain attitudes and behaviors if an individual makes the numbers and exceeds the goals. If that individual goes against the company's culture, is unwilling to think and act like a team player, or undermines the cohesiveness of the team in any way, then she needs to be removed. Otherwise, there is a risk that the cancer of cultural incompatibility will spread and potentially ruin the health of the organization.

For company leadership, making these tough people decisions, particularly when top talent is involved, is challenging. No one wants to let go of a strong performer who is boosting margins and bringing in profits (especially with the prospect that he could go to the competition). But for the health of the business and the effectiveness of the team for the long-term, it's the right thing to do.

Without mentioning names or restaurant chains, Federico thought of two examples of individuals whom he was willing to "stick by" and develop, instead of letting go. "In both of those cases, they turned out to be phenomenal leaders, and ultimately my bosses and my board came back and said, 'You know what, it turned out better than we would have anticipated.'" In time, they even became possible successors to upper management. That type of success story is not always the outcome. In fact, Federico has faced some criticism for "hanging onto people a little longer than I ought to," because of a conviction to "try my damnedest to help other people become successful."

The one thing he won't tolerate, however, is "cultural incompatibility," no matter how good a performer someone is. "If you are an ass, you can't work for me," he added bluntly.

For every disappointment, however, there have been many more successes, with people who rose to the challenge and gave their all in return for the opportunity to be part of a unique organization. Perhaps Federico sees himself in them: willing to look at things differently, trying things that have the potential to fail, and taking a chance on themselves.

TIPS FROM THE TITANS

- Look at things through a different lens to perceive the new and innovative, the undiscovered niche.
- "Right size" the business to avoid over-expansion and/or cannibalizing from other units.
- Seek to elevate the brand continuously, especially through employee training.
- Instill "pride of ownership" by establishing an emotional connection with the business.
- Help others to be successful, while stressing cultural compatibility.

Chapter Nine

Measure Your Progress at Every Step

> We have what we call our balanced scorecard from which we measure and operate the company. It's a tool we use, up and down the company.
>
> —Paul J. Diaz, CEO, Kindred Healthcare, Inc.

Successful businesses run by metrics and measures, gauging their progress toward strategic goals and milestones. These targets do not exist for their own sake; rather, they create a framework of achievement and accountability within the company and, externally, among all stakeholders. In the health-care industry, measures and metrics are crucial to delivering high-quality, effective care. Indeed, as health-care reform is implemented by policymakers and regulators, the health-care industry is turning increasingly to measures and metrics to judge the quality and efficiency of care delivery—everything from the average length of stay for patients admitted to the flow of individuals treated in the emergency department. Satisfaction surveys of patients and families provide feedback about the individual experience, which has a direct link to clinical outcomes. Patients who have good treatment experiences are more apt to follow doctors' orders, and thus improve their health status and reduce their need for readmission.

Health-care companies, of course, are not alone in their reliance on metrics and measures. Every company, large or small, must set performance targets and continuously gauge and track the distance to them. The challenge for entrepreneurs, however, is that they tend to be "big picture" idea people. Their natural talents gravitate toward envisioning a concept and imagining unique ways in which to serve the marketplace. Thus, the discipline of measuring and monitoring is not necessarily part of the typical entrepreneurial DNA. A business builder who has the vision to imagine what's possible *and* the acumen to gauge its achievement is a rare talent. Paul J. Diaz, CEO of Kindred Healthcare, Inc., is such an example.

For Diaz, an accountant and lawyer by training, measures and metrics have made the difference in turning around Kindred Healthcare, which emerged from Chapter 11 bankruptcy in 2001. The reorganization that followed led Kindred to become a Fortune 500 company, ranking 444 in 2012. Today, Kindred Healthcare employs seventy-eight thousand people in forty-six states and generates more than $6 billion in revenues (compared with $2.9 billion in 2001). This growth is even more impressive when Kindred's $700 million pharmacy division spinoff, PharMerica Corporation, is factored in.

Over the years, Kindred has experienced organic growth and expanded through new facility development and strategic acquisitions throughout the enterprise. Its performance has earned the organization numerous accolades, including being named one of the most-admired health-care companies by *Fortune* magazine. Diaz, who has served as CEO of Kindred Healthcare since 2004, has received his share of praise as well; he has been named one of the 100 Most Influential People in Healthcare five times and one of the top 25 Minority Executives in Healthcare three times by *Modern Healthcare* magazine. *Hispanic* magazine also honored him as one of the 25 Best Latinos in business.

Although such praise is impressive, even more notable are Diaz's discipline and deep commitment to hard data, measuring results and linking the measures to his and his team's reward systems. Measuring results is also critical to driving culture and behaviors, as well as allocating human and financial capital—important jobs for any business leader or entrepreneur. He revealed that part of his leadership thinking in a profile in *CEO Q* magazine, in which he remarked, "My advice for the up and coming is to broaden your skill-sets, learn the operations, the finance, and the customers."[1]

Although business builders may not necessarily share his background, which tends to be more methodical and analytical than that of others we've profiled, the skills Diaz demonstrates comprise a valuable tool kit for business builders (and/or their teams) to possess. At the same time, his reliance on what might be described as the cold, hard facts of performance is enhanced and balanced by a softer side: true passion for the business, a trait broadly shared by successful entrepreneurs. For Diaz, passion is exhibited in being of service to others, a value he learned at a very young age.

Where Many Gifts Are Given

As a young boy growing up in the Miami area in a first-generation Cuban-American family, Diaz was strongly and positively influenced by his grandfather, a surgeon who had once worked for former Cuban President Fulgencio Batista, who was overthrown by Fidel Castro. His grandfather stressed upon young Diaz the importance of education and excellence, delivered in a favorite line of advice, which shaped Paul's future: "To those who have great gifts come great responsibilities." With his grandfather and his uncle as role models (his father left the family when Diaz was very young), Diaz set his sights on success and making a difference in the lives of others.

Another positive influence was scouting, and Diaz eventually earned the top rank of Eagle Scout, which taught him values, teamwork, and leadership. It is no coincidence that the lessons Diaz cited from his scouting days were setting and achieving goals and taking a disciplined approach. (He's not alone; former Eagle Scouts can be found in the ranks of corporate executives, sports figures, and politicians.) "That experience really helped me a lot in life," added Diaz, who today is an ardent supporter of scouting and received the Good Scout Award from the Boy Scouts of America in 2012. "Scouting has been an incredible influence for a lot of people, particularly those who grow up in middle-class and lower-middle-class backgrounds."

Interestingly, Diaz's Eagle Scout project presaged his future career: he set up a volunteer program at a hospital where his mother worked in administration. In addition, Diaz held early jobs in the hospital that took him across the operation, from the pharmacy to the emergency room, seeing firsthand how health-care organizations are run. The best learning experience, however, may have been his job as an interpreter for the hospital administrator. "I always tell the story to my [Kindred Healthcare] teammates, that one of my earliest experiences about how to be a good health-care executive was working for the administrator of the hospital, who twice a week walked the floors of that hospital and visited every single patient," Diaz said. "Sixty percent of the patients in this hospital—the Kendall Regional Medical Center [near Miami]—were Cuban, and the administrator didn't speak Spanish. So I went along with him as his interpreter. I got a chance to see health care, not only from the supply room, radiology department, and pharmacy departments, but also from a guy who really understood how to make it very customer-oriented. That was the very personal side of delivering good health care...which made a lasting impression on me."

Diaz's conclusion from that young age, which he still demonstrates in his own leadership today, is that the best health-care organizations are those in which the CEO isn't confined to his office, but is on the floor and talking to nurses, patients, and families—"making sure everybody is getting what they need to get people home and get people well."

This observation does not apply only to health care. Across all industries and businesses, "management by wandering around"—a term that was popularized, in part, by management guru Tom Peters—encourages managers to be out among the employees, whether on the factory floor or among the cubicles. Free-flowing discussions with employees, as well as customers and vendors, yield valuable insights into how things are going and what can be improved. As other business builders shared from their early experiences (for example, Bill Marriott, who visited individual restaurants with his father and, later in his career, was known to show up at his hotel properties unannounced), such hands-on leadership fosters a connection with the team.

It's All About the Team

Although the Kindred Healthcare success story is often attributed to Diaz as the CEO, he quickly gives credit to those whom he sees as most responsible: the team. "I'm blessed that I've surrounded myself with really smart people," Diaz said. "Among the key leadership traits are having enough humility while also being self-assured enough that you can listen to your board, you can listen to your teammates, and you can surround yourself with true partners. Organizations benefit from that. Conversely, if you think you've got to be the smartest guy in the room, which often no one is, people get themselves in a lot of trouble."

THE STRENGTH OF BEING A TEAM LEADER

As the saying goes, "A chain is only as strong as the weakest link." In any organization, and particularly in an entrepreneurial one that is sharply focused on strategic goals to grow and expand the business, the way to have strong "links" is to recruit, train, and retain the best people for the team. As observed in earlier chapters, the objective is not to look for superstar solo artists who are in it only for themselves and what they can accomplish, but rather to have intelligent, gifted, and highly motivated team players. That attitude starts with the leader. Organizations looking to accelerate growth or that are in need of a turnaround require leaders who make a measurable difference in guiding and inspiring their teams.

(continued)

The entrepreneurial leaders who are most likely to become titans are those who foster collaboration toward the common good. They champion the creation of an environment and hire those who have strong collaboration skills. In addition, they put systems in place to make sure that all efforts ultimately benefit the customer—whether a guest in a restaurant or hotel, a patient in a hospital, or even a country in need of infrastructure development.

Keeping the customer satisfied is the job of every single employee. Think of an airline, in which employees who connect with customers via telephone, in the airport terminal, and on board the aircraft, as well as those behind the scenes, contribute directly to a traveler's experience. Successful execution doesn't happen automatically. It takes a leader with a vision who is able to communicate the goals broadly throughout the organization, providing a common purpose that can unify the team.

In health care, a team approach involves an interdisciplinary group of physicians, nurses, case managers, pharmacists, physical and rehabilitation therapists, social workers, and other clinicians. Team members move out of the silos of their individual practices because they must act as a cohesive unit to be patient centered. In health care, the bottom line is always about clinical outcomes for the patient.

"I don't see how we can possibly be successful if we are not producing good clinical outcomes—in the way that physicians practice in our hospitals and nursing and rehabilitation centers, and the therapists and nurses, laboratory technicians, discharge planners, commercial payers, and even the patients' families [come together]. If we're not doing a good job, then the business model falls part," Diaz said. "Focus on your customers. Take care of your people. Those are the principle drivers of your business results."

Putting the team first highlights the paradox of being an entrepreneur. On one hand, you must possess a healthy ego to undertake the incredible challenge of building a business that differentiates itself from the competition. Whatever "better mousetrap" you are offering to the marketplace, you need tremendous self-confidence to project the belief that your new service, offering, or product will make a meaningful difference to the consumer. On the other hand, you must be able to step back and bring in the best that a team has to offer. This means seeking out opinions and feedback from others and listening to what they have to say. As an entrepreneur, you may be gifted at generating ideas—but certainly not every idea.

During discussions, critiques should not be viewed or delivered as being personal. Emotional maturity among business builders requires compartmentalization of one's ego, being able to take a step back to absorb and process feedback without feeling challenged. If you are the entrepreneur/founder who identifies closely with the business, this can be difficult because you believe that you are the best qualified to determine the course for the organization and to lead the journey toward specific goals. Without empowerment of the team, however, innovation and improvement become stymied, which undermines the drive to continuously improve organizational excellence.

All of this highlights the importance of the entrepreneur who champions the team in authentic and discernible ways. Thus, for an entrepreneur to become a titan, she must have enough confidence to start on the journey and also enough humility to get out of the way of others whose input and participation is critical to growing and scaling the business.

Monitoring and Measuring Progress

It's no surprise, given his background and the business that he's in, that Diaz's discussion returned frequently to monitoring and measuring. Kindred Healthcare has articulated its value proposition through a strategy it calls "Continue the Care," with stated objectives of: providing superior clinical outcomes and quality care with a patient-centered approach that is disciplined and transparent; lowering costs by reducing lengths of stay in acute-care hospitals and by successfully transitioning patients to their homes at the highest possible level of function; and reducing readmissions to hospitals through integrated and interdisciplinary care management teams and protocols.

While goals are essential for providing a target and setting the direction toward which companies are moving, what remains most important is monitoring and measuring the incremental gains to achievement of those objectives and rewarding performance when it is achieved. "Over the last decade, we've not only built the company into a premier provider of health-care services in our space, but also one that has tripled in size and improved significantly along the metrics that we look at," Diaz said.

Its balanced scorecard metrics look across the operation to measure such things as employee and executive turnover, quality and service, growth, efficiency, capital, and organizational excellence. "This is where I tend to be the more disciplined, process-oriented guy," Diaz added. "We look at people scores, turnover, employee satisfaction, retention rate. We look at patient outcomes and clinical outcomes as measured by a number of standards used throughout health-care services, as well as customer satisfaction scores."

For example, its hospitals track year-to-year performance, which has yielded proof positive of its efforts to improve patient-care outcomes. In the area of customer service, its metrics drill into such factors as call light response, coordination between shifts, and pain management. As the Kindred Healthcare example shows, performance metrics gain meaning with granularity. A company doesn't just set a goal such as quality improvement without also identifying the components or initiatives that will move the needle. For a hospital, that might mean reducing the incidence of infections; for a manufacturer or a consumer business, quality will obviously be identified and articulated differently. The overall commonality is the importance of looking at the specifics and not just the generalities. In this way, a company can better allocate its resources and determine those activities and innovations that truly make a difference to the achievement of a goal—and, ultimately, the bottom line.

Another use of metrics is to keep teammates informed about the results of their efforts. People are more likely to go the extra mile when they know that what they do matters—and that someone is watching. Kindred Healthcare, for example, disseminates information such as data on patient experience and satisfaction: in 2011, nearly 70 percent of patients were discharged in less than thirty days, and 92 percent would recommend the organization to others to receive care. "That's where I start when I think about our value proposition for patients: if we're really successful with our people and successful with our patients, our clinical outcomes and customer service outcomes will really drive organic growth," Diaz said.

In addition, cost management and efficiency improvement drive savings, which are revealed in measures such as costs per patient day, which is tracked in every operating division. That, in turn, helps to determine how efficient the organization is in managing its capital. And, with greater transparency around that data, more accountability is built into the organization. These same metrics also drive the company's rewards and bonus plan, linking compensation with performance, which is a win–win for the organization and for the team members who are accountable for the results achieved.

"Organizational excellence is a constant. How are we going to do things better next year than we did this year? That's how you keep people engaged, too," Diaz remarked.

Building Value

For every organization, regardless of its industry or business niche, the objective is to create value. Although that may be defined differently depending upon whether an entrepreneur is expanding a restaurant chain or running a health-care company, the commonality is the importance of knowing how value will be determined in the marketplace. "Great businesses make money, but a great business has to start with creating value for customers, and that means innovating," Diaz said. "Whether you are making cars or taking care of patients or building airplanes—whatever you're doing—you have to be good at it and you have to stay ahead [of the competition] and get better at it."

Building value goes hand in hand with talent development so that a company has the right people on board to effect change. When the emphasis is on value creation, people can become truly passionate about what they do, without the negative side effect of emotions (especially ego), which can undermine the process of rational, fact-based decision making.

Thus, building a team and building a culture are foundational to every enterprise; one cannot be separated from the other. Values-based goals that are customer-centric (or, in the case of Kindred, patient-centric) motivate people to focus on what truly makes a difference in the marketplace. In that way, the emphasis is not just on profitability (as important as that is to building a sustainable business) but also about establishing a lasting legacy that will be communicated and passed on through systems and processes that reinforce culture.

Legacy and values also play an important role in executive succession, so that the leadership bench of talent being developed now is steeped in the enduring principles that people come to associate with a company and its culture. It's all about the performance-based discipline, continuously measured and monitored, and the lasting legacy that lives on beyond the tenure of any one executive, driving entrepreneurial growth and sustainability.

TIPS FROM THE TITANS

- ☛ Set goals and continuously measure the distance to them with precise and meaningful metrics, and link success on those measures to your reward system.
- ☛ Track performance year over year and within divisions or departments to gauge what truly "moves the needle" toward the ultimate objectives.

☞ Balance reliance on the hard facts of data with the softer side of passion for the business.

☞ Strengthen and develop the team with the best talent, but never rely totally on "star players"; a team mind-set is paramount.

☞ Foster a culture of value creation through a collaborative team approach focused on improving the customer experience.

Chapter Ten

Be Mindful of the Shadow You Cast

> *Integrity is like your shadow...When you walk out into the sunshine, it is there for everybody to see.*
>
> —John Robbins, Founder, American Residential
> Mortgage Corporation and Past President,
> Mortgage Bankers Association

When a storm hits, most people's inclination is to head for safety. Literally or figuratively, it's best to be in the basement, away from the fury. In business, a storm of another type—such as a crisis caused by economic, safety, environmental, or other issues—often prompts the same "duck and cover" response. Only someone with courage and stamina can face the storm head on. These stalwart and notable few willingly stand exposed to the storm, taking a lashing (including from the media and the general public) in order to provide a clear-headed perspective or to calm irrational fears. Leadership that is developed throughout one's career becomes tested and defined during times of crisis.

THE WISDOM OF TITANS

The biggest storm of recent years was unquestionably the financial crisis of 2008–2009, a meltdown that can be traced directly to an implosion of the housing market, which was compounded by overly inflated property values and a rash of poor-quality loans, including nondocumented mortgages that did not require the borrower to prove income or other financial resources. These lending practices were part of a bigger mess known as subprime: simply stated, too much money loaned to too many people who did not have the means to afford their mortgages. Furthermore, subprime and even higher-quality loans were sometimes used to finance 90 percent or even 100 percent of the purchase price. When property values declined, people could no longer refinance their way to a stopgap solution.

Further compounding the problem, mortgages of varying qualities (prime, subprime, and levels in between) were packaged together and securitized, meaning they were converted into investment securities, such as collateralized debt obligations, and sold to investors. When housing prices dropped, foreclosures skyrocketed, and the risks of subprime lending were exposed, the value of these securities plummeted. It was a classic domino effect. A sizeable portion of the blame, as well as the scrutiny, fell on the residential mortgage banking industry.

Into that fray stepped John M. Robbins, who has worked in residential mortgage finance since 1972 and, most notably, founded American Residential Mortgage Corporation, which grew to become one of the largest independent mortgage banks in the United States. He also founded American Residential Investment Trust in 1997 and then American Mortgage Network in 2001. By 2007, he was in another position: president of the Mortgage Bankers Association, becoming a voice of reason about the housing crisis and testifying before Congress and other state and federal lawmakers.

For Robbins, the storm of the housing crisis was not a period during which he should take cover and wait it out, but rather a time to step up and demonstrate leadership. As he saw it, that tempest was exactly the time for the mortgage banking industry to be proactive. "The best thing you can do is become part of the solution," he advised. "What that means is facing your adversaries. I walked the halls of Congress for almost a solid year, meeting every congressman and every senator who would see me, every member of the Senate and the House Banking and Finance Committees. I was letting them know exactly what was going on and, more importantly, bringing solutions to the table."

Certainly no entrepreneur wants to be thrust into the position of spokesperson for an industry under fire. There are times, however, when such a role is unavoidable; problems reach a crescendo and the most reputable thing to do is step up and speak out. In Robbins's case, he willingly took on the role because of his longevity in the business and his standing as a leader. Furthermore, he felt strongly about the issues involved, such as loan officer licensing, increased fiduciary responsibility on the part of lenders, and a stronger commitment to consumers and their well-being. Rather than being focused on the fees generated by loans, Robbins believed the priority for mortgage lending institutions was to create reasonable expectations on the part of customers, where they make mortgage payments over a period of time. This was the message he wanted to deliver inside and outside the industry.

Underscoring Robbins's leadership was a deep-seated belief

in a particular trait that crosses all industries and business niches: integrity. Integrity demands that a leader adhere to high standards of professional and ethical conduct above the minimum of the letter of the law. Integrity creates and reinforces an organizational culture in which people serve goals that go beyond making this month's or this quarter's numbers. Trying to wring every dime out of the profits (such as focusing only on writing the maximum number of loans every month, regardless of credit quality or the suitability of the loan to the consumer) is an unsustainable game that leads to poor decisions and untenable risks. With integrity, however, thinking shifts from "How much lending can we do?" to "Why are we doing what we're doing and what is the long-term impact?"

TOUGH TIMES CALL FOR STRONG LEADERS

When a business or industry faces severe challenges, organizations need leaders who not only weather the storms, but also face them. Leadership and taking responsibility go hand in hand, setting an example of acceptable behavior and taking accountability when problems need to be addressed.

What makes such a leader, one who is able to step up to the plate during challenging times instead of hiding and obfuscating? As with much of the leadership discussions thus far in the book, it comes down to character. A leader who can take on the challenges tomorrow is the one who can set the rules and the example today. This means leading others and managing the business with integrity, and doing the right thing for the long term instead of focusing only on short-term gain.

(continued)

Strong, accountable leaders make sure others follow the rules and adhere to the culture, especially when competitive pressures raise the temptation to act in a different way. The importance of staying the course is reinforced in every communication and interaction.

Leaders who can endure the challenges can be found among those who build teams of like-minded people, the team players who embrace the values and take the high road instead of the easier path that presents itself at times. That is the only way to build a sustainable business and create the kind of leadership, both internally and externally, that can ride out the storm and step into the hurricane when necessary.

The Integrity "Shadow"

As a leadership quality, true integrity speaks for itself; the aura of this positive attribute will spread far and wide. Conversely, if a leader lacks integrity, that negative aspect creates toxic seepage that poisons opportunities and makes for costly cleanup after the fact. How others perceive a leader's integrity precedes every interaction and colors every conversation. As the old saying goes: reputation takes a lifetime to build, but only a moment to destroy. This is a strong caution for the entrepreneur who is establishing a business in a highly competitive marketplace, in which there are numerous temptations to cut corners or to rationalize a shortsighted action as something everyone is doing. In order to develop and maintain integrity, the entrepreneur simply must take the higher road, without exception.

When Robbins speaks to his employees about integrity, he compares it to one's shadow. In the dark, the shadow can be hidden. Sooner or later, though, a person has to come out of hiding and into the bright light of attention. Then the shadow of integrity is visible for all to see. "If you have integrity, if you are an ethical, moral human being...then people trust you," he said.

Such lofty words are hollow unless there is action to back them up. Integrity's proof, one might say, is in the experience of it. "In the organizations that I have built, we do not hide our financial statements. We do not hide variances from plan," Robbins added. "Every one of our employees knows actually where we sit all of the time. As I like to say to them, 'There is no such thing as a hole in the end of the boat.' By that I mean, we all sink or swim together."

In an organization, a weak spot or troubled area can taint the entire operation. Where ethical or moral breaches or just plain bad business decisions are concerned, an enterprise can very quickly face mounting troubles.

Within the mortgage banking industry, a breakdown occurred when loan origination became distanced and even divorced from a lender's own balance sheet. That disconnect created a lack of accountability on the part of loan officers who were lending as much as possible, because it was none of their concern whether or not the borrower could afford the payments. When the loans were packaged and sold to other investors, the loans quickly became someone else's problem, an attitude that was endemic in mortgage brokering.

Robbins's organizations, however, were known for a significantly higher degree of accountability because the objective was to create a sustainable and credible business that was ultimately responsible for the loan portfolio. Even if that meant forgoing the most aggressive players on the teams who could really drive loan volume, Robbins preferred to have a more cohesive and experienced group that appreciated integrity. They willingly worked that much harder and spent considerably more time finding the right customer, rather than trying to write loans for every person who came in the door. The compensation plan reflected and reinforced that culture as well, with commissions and bonuses tied to loan performance plus other incentives that were reasonable and conveyed the importance of confidence, trust, and respect.

There is a direct correlation to other industries, as well: integrity is not simply an inspiring word in a mission statement. It must become a pillar that supports everything from business strategy to compensation plans. The behavior that the leader wants to see in his organization must be stipulated, emulated, and recognized. Typically, such behavior translates into being closely aligned with the customer; acting in the best interest of consumers (with products or services that ultimately take into consideration their well-being) promotes integrity and accountability. For Robbins, this was a lesson learned early in life.

Early Lessons in What to Do—and Not Do—in Business

Growing up in Phoenix, Arizona, Robbins gained his first education in business and the importance of customer service at his grandfather's stationery and office equipment business. From grade school into his high school years (roughly from ages ten to sixteen), Robbins watched his grandfather build and run his business. A strong connection, Robbins saw, went both ways: his grandfather took great pains to serve the needs of his clients; his customers, in turn, showed "absolute devotion and loyalty to him." Later on, in the mortgage business, Robbins would place a high priority on servicing customers with the right loans for their needs. The takeaway for entrepreneurs, once again, is in getting the cultural component correct. Such affinities do not just happen, but are determined by the priorities of the leader and affirmed by the actions that start at the top.

"Building great teams is important, but I think customer service—the way you treat your customers—is more important," Robbins observed. "If you concentrate solidly on creating a dynamic employee base that is impassioned, empowered, and believes in the plan; if they like the company culture and trust the executives because there is integrity there, then they will work their hearts out. If you treat your customers the same way, the customers will reward you with their loyalty." With those two objectives accomplished—an empowered team and a loyal customer base—shareholder value will follow.

After the early lessons learned at his grandfather's store, Robbins's personal story continued with enlistment in the military in the mid-1960s and then selection and training for U.S. Army Intelligence, serving in Korea along the Demilitarized Zone. Post-discharge, he attended college part time while he worked, starting off in the promotions department for a regional shopping center. The general manager above him was fairly young, which meant opportunities for advancement would not materialize any time soon. Beyond the apparent impatience (which is a fairly common trait among entrepreneurs), Robbins recognized that what he really wanted was to find "an industry that I thought I could grow in." His mother, a realtor, suggested mortgage banking. Robbins was intrigued by the possibility, and was subsequently hired by a mortgage finance company that ranked third or fourth in the country. After learning the mortgage business "from the ground up," Robbins pursued other opportunities, including the purchase of a mortgage banking company from a multistate thrift, which he turned into a national operation.

These experiences enabled Robbins, who was about thirty years old at that time, to not only be a student of the mortgage banking industry, but also of business in general. His experience echoed that of other titans profiled; they looked beyond their particular industries and market niches to observe trends and learn lessons broadly. For Robbins, the breadth of study included personal lessons as well; chief among them was how a leader should act—and not act. The point was brought home in a comment made by the wife of a company executive at a sales conference, who remarked that she wasn't going to participate in a particular event because she didn't want mix to with "the little people." Hearing the remark, Robbins was floored.

"Here was a woman who, theoretically, could be a great asset to her husband, and yet she took what was absolutely in my mind the most destructive, reverse tactic that she could take," he said. "She was unapproachable and felt eminently better than the people who worked so hard to make her husband successful."

This incident, along with other experiences and observations, influenced Robbins' thinking about leadership, whether as a manager within an organization or, later on, as an entrepreneur and industry leader. He summed it up as "knowing the kind of leader I wanted to be." This lesson spans all types of companies, industries, and leadership positions, whether someone works for an organization or builds her own. For the entrepreneur who is understandably preoccupied with establishing and growing a business, defining one's leadership principles cannot be neglected or left to default. At a relatively young age, Robbins took pains to define his leadership, long before he occupied the C-suite. The backdrop for his musings was a scenario in an elevator.

"There are two kinds of CEOs who get on an elevator. There is the CEO who rides to his top floor while standing in the corner, never saying anything to anybody—just staring at his newspaper," Robbins explained. "Then there is the CEO who gets on the elevator and intentionally says hello to everybody. He looks them in the eye."

Even more important than the CEO's behavior is the reaction among the employees. Those who ride the elevator with the second CEO are far more likely to be motivated and engaged. "They'll say, 'I just rode up the elevator with the [CEO] of the company. What a nice guy he is,'" Robbins added. That connection will go a long way toward team building and reinforcing a culture of mutual respect.

Through his career in the mortgage business, Robbins has also learned industry-specific lessons, such as loan securitization. While working at a thrift institution, Robbins was given the dual tasks of creating a nationwide loan company and improving the quality of underwriting to meet securitization standards. Securitization of quality loan creates investment products and allows reasonable risks to be hedged. Later in his career, however, Robbins observed alarming practices in the industry of subprime lending and other poor-quality loans, which could be passed off to institutional investors through securitization.

Control of His Own Destiny

There is a strong commonality among many entrepreneurs that sets them on a path to establish their own company rather than work for someone else. This trait may emerge early on, or it may surface more gradually over time—sometimes after success in a traditional corporate environment. For Robbins, the entrepreneurial catalyst was sparked after he worked for four banking institutions. Although they provided invaluable experiences, in the end they proved disappointing, either because upper management lacked an understanding of the mortgage business or credit quality was not a priority, which translated into instability. This brought Robbins to a crossroads in his career path and to the decision to head in a different direction to be, as he put it, "in control of my own destiny."

The first venture was American Residential Mortgage Corporation, which he took public in 1993 and then sold to the former Chase Manhattan Bank in 1994. Afterward, he took an early retirement with all the trappings: yacht, fishing excursions, golf five times a week. "While it was okay, it was not a great steady diet," Robbins said. In short, it was time to go back to work.

For most entrepreneurs, the drive to create businesses is not satisfied by achieving success or attaining a financial goal. There is real joy and passion in the execution of the plan, in building a business out of nothing but a concept. That urge to create and expand a business, in turn, generates opportunities for others. Entrepreneurs large and small should recognize the important role they play in the advancement of the economy and especially in job creation.

Robbins's next venture was in 1997, with the creation of

American Residential Investment Trust, a real estate investment trust (REIT), an investment opportunity that had always intrigued him. Although the REIT performed satisfactorily and weathered a downturn that eliminated many competitors, Robbins was convinced it was time to return to his roots with the creation of a nationwide wholesale mortgage banking company that ultimately became American Mortgage Network (AmNet). To gain backing for the planned conversion from a REIT to a mortgage company, Robbins went back to the very first lessons learned at his grandfather's store: talk to the customers and serve their needs.

"I personally called every shareholder who owned five thousand or more shares [of the REIT]," he explained. "It was a gargantuan task." But this was precisely the kind of personal service that made the difference between acceptance and rejection. At a special shareholders' meeting, one large shareholder, who had earlier indicated he was going to oppose the plan, switched his vote in favor. With that, the company obtained more than the necessary 66.67 percent approval and was able to proceed with the conversion.

The point of the story and the takeaway for other entrepreneurs is the importance of personalization. It's not enough for a leader to have a "fire in the belly" to create something; the plan, by design, must involve others. The strategy extends beyond the internal team to external stakeholders, including vendors, customers, and, in some cases, shareholders. "I truly felt the proposed conversion to a mortgage bank was our best opportunity to create shareholder value in the future. The fact I was able to successfully sell that plan to the existing investors in the REIT was a direct result of the personal calls from the CEO of the company," Robbins said.

After AmNet was sold in 2005 to Wachovia, a three-year noncompete agreement took Robbins temporarily out of the mortgage business as a banker, but not out of the industry. Instead, as this story comes full circle, he took a position with the Mortgage Bankers Association at what proved to be a crucial time for the industry. This was the heyday of the mortgage business, in which lenders across the industry were writing loans to people who lacked the income base to take on the level of debt they were assuming. (Although AmNet was involved in subprime lending in 2004, by 2005 it was out of that business. "I couldn't stand the product. It just didn't fit our culture," Robbins said. "We were a high-integrity culture and the subprime business was not. The two just did not go together.") Across the industry, however, the name of the game was rampant loan generation with not much internal policing about the quality of the loans being written.

"It was just nonsensical. Loans were being made to people who had no poker chips on the table," Robbins said. "They essentially had 100 percent loan to value [meaning the loan was for the full value of the home at the time].... This was a disastrous business, so I started to speak up publicly about it."

In columns for *Mortgage Banking Magazine* that Robbins wrote in 2005, he warned about the "train wreck that was coming," foreseeing "that we as an industry will pay a disastrous price" because of subprime and other poor-quality loans. As he saw it, the real estate market had undergone tremendous appreciation in value and could not continue its exponential growth. It only made sense that the cyclical real estate industry would undergo an adjustment; otherwise, how would new buyers be able to afford a home? "I said, 'I see heavy storm clouds ahead and ... sooner or later, this thing is going to happen,'" he recalled. The magnitude of the fallout—not only a bursting of the housing bubble, but the resulting financial crisis—turned out to be far greater than he or most people ever envisioned.

Since the crisis, the mortgage banking industry has elevated lending standards and improved consumer education and customer service. Although the housing market remains under pressure, particularly in some hard-hit regions of the United States, there are signs of improvement. Little wonder, then, that Robbins sees opportunities to go back into the business, this time with a partnership to form a new mortgage origination company focusing on the wholesale and retail markets. "I always felt that the time to create or buy was at the bottom of the cycle," Robbins said.

Downsizing in the mortgage finance industry over the past few years has reduced competition, while the current mix of loan programs is producing valuable mortgage assets at affordable prices. Although times may be tough for a few more years, for companies with a disciplined culture and the fiscal means, there are opportunities to grow and expand. "Now is the time to salvage your company, grow your branches, grow your infrastructure, grow your company, so that when the normal market does return, you have the resources in place to take advantage of that, rather than waiting until you know that the market has turned," Robbins added.

Virtually all businesses endure some cyclicality, a waxing and waning of opportunities, and periods of growth and then retrenchment. Through these phases what does not change are certain immutable qualities: solid leadership, a team orientation, a strong customer focus, and one potent word that can make all the difference—integrity.

BE MINDFUL OF THE SHADOW YOU CAST

- ☞ Uphold integrity at all times, knowing that the "shadow" you cast is visible to all.
- ☞ Recognize that a crisis tests and elevates leadership. Do not shrink from opportunities to take a stand and advocate for positive change.
- ☞ Avoid the shortcuts and quickest paths to profits that may involve too much risk and prove dangerous in the long run.
- ☞ Focus on customer service by providing products that truly improve the well-being of consumers.
- ☞ Seek opportunities to expand and grow your business during downturns and other challenging times.

Chapter Eleven

Make the 2 Percent Difference

Before you complete a task, pause for two seconds and ask yourself 'If I did 2 percent more, would it make a difference?'"

—William A. "Bill" Jensen, CEO, Intrawest

The difference between an entrepreneur and a titan is not determined by personal net worth or the size of the company's bottom line. External measures, no matter how impressive, are not the defining characteristics. Some of the true differentiators can be categorized as business skills; as discussed in previous chapters, these include developing a team, executing a plan, and staying focused on those things that move the levers of a successful operation. Others are personal, including drive, discipline, and integrity. Among the cream-of-the-crop entrepreneurs, the ones who reach the pinnacle of success, there is another trait that is part personality and part discipline. Rooted in early life experiences, it sometimes shows itself as work ethic, but really goes deeper than that. Bill Jensen, CEO of Intrawest, which develops and manages leading ski resorts in the United States and Canada as well as other worldwide destination properties, calls it "the 2 percent difference."

It comes down to this: entrepreneurs who become titans never look at a task as something to check off a list. They consider why the job needs to be accomplished, what impact it makes on the client or consumer, and what else can be done to improve such things as quality, efficiency, or satisfaction. It might be described in all the usual clichés of "going the extra mile" or "crossing t's and dotting i's." Terminology doesn't matter; results do.

"I have always done that in my life," Jensen said of his "2 percent rule." "It really creates attention to detail in my mind. For example, even with the smallest tasks, when I finish I ask myself, 'What would be the 2 percent difference that I could add to this?'"

Giving that little extra doesn't necessarily mean working harder or even more; in fact, it can be part of good efficiency and time management that actually reduces the amount of time and attention that tasks require because it incorporates what Jensen calls "working in an appropriate way." The 2 percent difference may eliminate the need to go back to fix or change something. Moreover, it often improves one's own satisfaction with the job to be done. "It's one of those concepts that I try to share with people as a way to look at life," Jensen added. "And I apply it personally to everything. It is constantly in the back of my head. It's second nature for me to say, 'Alright, what's the 2 percent rule here?'"

As with many entrepreneurs, Jensen learned these formative lessons early in life. The oldest of three, he recalled growing up in a household where dinner table conversation often related stories of his parents' interactions with people at work. His father, an aeronautical engineer, worked on projects for NASA, including control rockets for the Apollo space capsule and the lunar landing vehicle. His mother reentered the workforce when Jensen and his brother and sister were young, and worked in human resources, including for Hewlett-Packard. "I started to understand at an early age the role that people play in the success of an organization or a business," he added.

And he learned how each member contributes to the running of the household—Jensen and his siblings were assigned tasks such as washing cars by hand (a chore that Jensen still enjoys) and making their beds in the morning. (Jensen's wife teases him about his discipline of making the bed as soon as they get up.) In time, the 2 percent difference reinforced a work ethic that, as with other titans profiled in this book, was developed early on through hard work. During high school, Jensen spent summers doing grading and landscaping work for neighbors in Southern California; as a college student, first at Menlo College and then at Pepperdine University, he poured cement driveways and swimming pool decks. The value of having done that hard work has lasted throughout his professional career. As he noted: "When people ask me, 'Can you get my son a job?' my response is, 'Maybe manual labor will be better.'...I never shied away from hard work or a challenge. Those seeds were planted early."

The overarching lessons from Jensen's early experiences are self-evident: extra effort pays off not only in a job well done, but in honing a discipline that looks beyond good enough to greatness. It is the attention to detail that others notice, particularly when it comes to customer service. Among entrepreneurs who ultimately become titans, this orientation influences how they lead others—not by directive, but by example. Ingraining this kind of attitude in the team translates into customer satisfaction and repeat business.

Long before these leadership days, however, the

entrepreneur-in-the-making must choose her path, which can be as obvious as joining the family business or can involve, as it did for Jensen, a more circuitous route of self-discovery.

Finding Career Affinity

Typically, during a person's life, there is a fifteen- to twenty-year window during which one's professional identity is established. The process is revelatory, as initial hints become stronger evidence. Jensen described being "a bit in the dark" about what he wanted to do with his life until he went on a skiing trip after college with friends at Mammoth Mountain in Southern California, after which he walked into the personnel office and asked for a job. His plan was to work at the ski resort that winter, making $2.50 an hour, while figuring out the next step in his life. As the season wound down, however, Jensen was still without a long-term career plan (much to his parents' dismay); his default decision was to stay on. Given his previous experience doing concrete work, he was hired for a major construction project at the resort. The work ethic he developed earlier and his willingness to make the 2 percent difference impressed his boss. After only nine months he was promoted to lift supervisor, a job Jensen viewed as "getting paid to ski every day, so there was nothing wrong with that," especially because his salary doubled. More important for his long-term development, Jensen began to supervise people, drawing from what he called "affinity skills" that went back to his college days when he helped put together study groups. Little did he know at that time, but this ski resort job would lead not only to his career, but to considerable success in the future.

Once again, we find evidence that a titan found his path early in life, through a combination of good luck, coincidence, and willingness to work hard. As Jensen's story shows, it's not simply a matter of opening the proverbial door when opportunity knocks; recognition of opportunity, being willing to stretch to take on new tasks and responsibilities, and putting forth the extra effort to distinguish yourself are even more important. Another element, as Jensen described it, is finding one's affinity: for a young man who had spent summers doing manual labor outdoors, who loved to ski, and who had some natural leadership talent, the makings of a career in ski resorts began to be assembled from those initial pieces in an interesting way (although his parents still thought he should get a "real job").

Early in his career, Jensen found a role model in Dave McCoy, who founded Mammoth Mountain, whom he described as "very engaged, very involved, and very connected to all of the employees." Watching McCoy in action in a business that dealt mostly with happy customers who were enjoying a sport they loved, Jensen recognized his plan for the future. At the age of twenty-three, Jensen decided that, by the time he turned forty, he would run a ski resort. "I didn't tell my parents, I didn't tell my friends, I just made that commitment," he added. After another eighteen months at Mammoth, Jensen realized he needed to broaden his skill set and his horizon, which started a progression through the ski industry. He spent seven or eight years in the outdoor operating environment side of the business, and then five or six years on the marketing side. Jensen's development was deliberate, as it should be for any entrepreneur—particularly those who aim to become titans. Knowing every facet of the business develops competencies and broadens knowledge. Certain areas will, of course, be more of a natural fit or simply of greater interest. With greater breadth of understanding comes insight into how to improve a business model or find an underserved niche.

As Jensen advanced through the industry, he distinguished himself as a business builder who could take an idea through execution and a successful outcome. "If you can build that track record by [successful execution] several times, it starts to become a habit for any person or leader," he advised. A person will know that he has advanced to the stage of "having arrived" in his career, Jensen added, by his ability to influence outcomes. "If you are invited to a meeting or if you are working on a project and your input or actions influence the outcome of that project, then you really do start to realize that you are adding value to the team or the organization."

Jensen also applied this outcomes-based thinking to his career development, evaluating opportunities on the basis of how a particular job would provide additional experience or advance his career, while also allowing him to contribute to the success of an organization. As a result, he reached his goal a year early: two weeks before his thirty-ninth birthday, he was running a ski resort. (From 1991 to 1997, he served as president of Fibreboard Resort Group, overseeing the executive management of three ski resorts in California: Northstar and Sierra at Tahoe, and Bear Mountain.) At the age of thirty-two, he was quoted for the first time in the *Wall Street Journal*. Upon reading the article, his mother called to congratulate him. "Yes, Mom," Jensen quipped. "I do have a real job." He shared that story many times in his career, including in 2008 when he was inducted into the Colorado Ski Hall of Fame; his parents were still alive and able to share the occasion with him. Afterward, he was surprised by the number of people who told him they'd had similar conversations with their own families over the years.

MAKE THE 2 PERCENT DIFFERENCE

This lighthearted story also provides some insight, particularly for younger entrepreneurs, that those who are closest to them may not always see their career development in the same way they do. Their families or close friends may have other hopes and expectations for them, such as having a "real job" or changing to an industry that is perceived to be more established, stable, or even prestigious. Staying true to your own ideals, while also keeping an open mind toward well-intentioned feedback and guidance, can be difficult; but even that bit of adversity can test a young entrepreneur in a way that either shakes her confidence or affirms that she is, indeed, on the right path.

Although it may look like "too much fun," as Jensen quipped, the statistics he cited on the U.S. ski industry show just how serious a business it is: sixty million visitors a year (on par with attendance figures for Major League Baseball); $6 billion a year for the operation or resort side of the business; and another $3 billion for equipment and clothing. Add in the real estate component and community development, and the economic impact becomes exponentially larger.

Jensen's career path followed the trajectory of the industry, which in the 1980s or 1990s included mostly companies with only one or two ski areas. By the mid-1990s, large resort companies dominated, and Jensen was part of their leadership. In 1997, he joined Vail Resorts Management Company as chief operating officer (COO) at its Breckenridge (Colorado) Ski Resort, and then became COO of Vail Mountain in 1999. In 2008, he was named CEO of Denver-based Intrawest, which has a network of resorts and ski destinations in North America, including Mont Tremblant, Steamboat, Winter Park, Snowshoe, and Stratton; a Canadian heli-skiing operation, which is the largest in the world; and a private resort club with locations around the world. Intrawest, which is the number-two owner/ operator of ski resorts in the United States based on revenues, behind Vail Resorts, employs about thirteen thousand people during the peak winter season and about forty-five hundred on a year-round basis.

With thirty-five years in the industry, Jensen views the consolidation of resort properties as evidence of the evolution of the business, which today must focus on the synergies created by portfolios of properties. "How do you provide the oversight, the direction, and the capital, and also [address] all the issues that really make this a much more complex business?" Jensen asked. The answer goes back to the example that the leader sets for the team.

Outwork Your Competitors

There are two basic ingredients to success: one is hard work, and the other is passion. The two are inextricably linked for the simple reason that it is hard, and perhaps even impossible, to give one's all with the kind of time and effort necessary to build and sustain a business without passion. With passion, though, the necessary hard work becomes not only endurable, but pleasurable. As other titans in this book demonstrated, when you are enthralled and energized by a business opportunity, there is ample motivation to do whatever it takes. "If you have the passion and ability to make the commitment and outwork your competitors, you are always going to have an advantage," Jensen said. "In hindsight, as I look back on my career, I think that axiom has been correct 99 percent of the time. Obviously, there are those occasions when, no matter how hard you work, it may not change the outcome, which is a disappointment, but nobody bats a thousand for a whole career."

Passion, as a potent driver of success, is not unique to a services business. "From my perspective, it is a key component of any business," Jensen said. "It doesn't matter whether you want to be a doctor or a dentist.... The common denominator that I have seen with people who are the most successful is passion for what they do." Passion translates into engagement, which is enhanced by a strong work ethic and the ability to work harder than everyone else, particularly the competition. Without these elements, the entrepreneur faces a difficult mountain to climb.

Another critical lesson is that good decision making takes solid information; thus, the wise leader tries to get as much input as possible. This can be a challenge for entrepreneurs who, by nature, tend to be a little fast on the trigger; they want to make decisions quickly and then move onto the next thing, and so they go with their gut and their instinct. The discipline of good decision making, particularly where strategic direction is involved, requires that you take all the time you can, as Jensen advised. Why make a decision on a Monday night when you might have a little more clarity and perspective on Tuesday morning? The bigger the organization, the more important it is not to make spontaneous decisions.

Mistakes and disappointments will happen, and yet also yield lessons that help prevent strategic or tactical missteps from being made twice. Even when it's difficult, this learning process is made more palatable when your passion is channeled into a particular niche or opportunity. "As I look at entrepreneurs and other successful businesspeople, I can always see a passion for some aspect [of what they do]. The passion can be around the product, the passion can be around the experience, or the passion can be around just the thrill of being in business," Jensen said.

Jensen's experiences also taught him that game-changing opportunities—the kind that accelerate a business forward—are rare, but they do happen. Therefore, leaders must keep their eyes open for them. "They don't come along every week, every month, or even every year," he advised. Most of the time, progress is incremental, sometimes faster or slower than others, but at a steady pace that the leader must maintain. As Jensen said, quoting a favorite saying, "Inch by inch, life's a cinch; yard by yard, life is hard."

Thus the real secret to success might come down to the most prosaic and basic of all advice: work hard and stay focused; be disciplined and committed. It sounds easy, but it's not—especially given the intensity and dedication that are required to maintain a high level of engagement over the long haul. Those who can, however, stand a far better chance than their competition to rise above the crowd.

ENTREPRENEURIAL DNA

Is entrepreneurship part of one's DNA or does it stem from a combination of factors? This is a question we have tried to address in this book by examining the professional lives and experiences of several leaders.

Based upon my own experiences, having built a global professional services firm that specializes in senior management recruitment and compensation as well as management consulting, and drawing upon the entrepreneurial titans whom I've had the privilege to meet and work with, I do believe that there is something to be said for entrepreneurial DNA. Business building starts internally

(continued)

and manifests externally. The germ of the idea may come from wanting to be the boss (or, more to the point, one's own boss), but titans cannot be motivated by ego or a sense of privilege.

Rooted in their psyche is a desire to serve, especially a customer base with which they identify. Their business proposition must be based upon a need that is either underserved or undiscovered. Their go-to-market plan must be based on satisfying customers with a product, service, or experience that exceeds expectations and benefits them in tangible and measurable ways.

Whether an organization is being built from the ground up or an enterprise is embarking on a growth plan or even a turnaround phase, a leader with an entrepreneurial mind-set knows what it takes to outpace the competition. In a more established company, the leader may be a few or several operating layers above the front line, but is never removed from it. The business-building leader understands that a close connection to the marketplace is a powerful way to gather the necessary intelligence, to make strategic decisions for the long term, and to course correct the plan that's now in place.

Yes, entrepreneurs are born. By nature and perhaps by nurture, particularly in their early experiences, they gain the vision, drive, and discipline to build and sustain a business. They differentiate themselves by their commitment and level of engagement, and their abilities to select, develop, and empower a team. Whether their name is on the door or they have been brought into an organization founded by someone else, these leaders provide the vision and spearhead the execution to take the operation to the next level and, ultimately, to build a legacy.

The Mentor

At virtually any industry conference, it's easy to see where Bill Jensen is: in the thick of the biggest crowd. By virtue of his years in the business and the kind of leader he is, Jensen attracts people who want to ask him a question, gain his perspective, and, very often, thank him for what he's done for them. Just as he once looked up to Dave McCoy, so others now look up to him—and largely because every interaction with him is so genuine. For Jensen, mentoring is a privilege.

Being a mentor within an organization helps to develop people who will, in turn, focus on achieving measurable results; but it doesn't stop there. Entrepreneurs who reach titan status contribute to people in their industry, those colleagues and direct reports who may spend a few years with their company before moving on to another opportunity. For the entrepreneur, the pattern is often recognizable as the same path she took in earlier days.

"The analogy I like to use is that, when we are in the achievement phase of our careers, we get to play quarterback. But when you become the business leader, you have to stop playing quarterback and you start coaching," Jensen said.

He looks back fondly on the years, particularly the period between ages thirty-five and forty when, as the quarterback of the operating team, he was "in every huddle and got to be part of every play." Then came his transition to coach, leaving someone else to the quarterback position. At that stage, Jensen's priorities shifted to attracting and retaining those players who wanted to be part of the team and giving them opportunities to develop and excel.

"Part of the legacy that I want to leave is I want people to say,

'He was a great mentor,'" Jensen said. Among his friends are leaders in other industries who are now in the same phase of their careers, who have transitioned from star player to coach. "And I admire them for it," he added.

Here is the final word on the wisdom of titans: the businesses they build are not all about them. Their success may be established in the moment, during part of a career time line, but the enduring value is realized only over the years and even decades, sometimes after they have stepped down from their positions of power. The wisdom of titans is articulated not as epitaph, but as epilogue: the businesses they built were so much the better because they were there, day in and day out—planning, strategizing, executing, and developing. Then, at the end of the day, the organization continued on with a talented team of other titans in the making.

TIPS FROM THE TITANS

- Identify the "2 percent difference" you can make to elevate your efforts and improve your outcomes.
- Develop a reputation for solid execution and for improving the outcomes in your organization.
- Seek out opportunities to build competencies and broaden your skill sets across various facets of the business.
- Outwork your competitors to gain and keep a strategic edge.
- Mentor others to build the business and establish a legacy.

Epilogue

The Differentiators

There are entrepreneurs, and then there are titans.

Within the business world, entrepreneurial skills encompass vision, strategy, and a host of abilities to turn a concept into a reality. Entrepreneurs are, by and large, idea people. They see opportunities where others do not or, perhaps more accurately, have not as yet. Entrepreneurs are driven by passion for what they do; no matter how much success they enjoy (and how well they are rewarded financially), business building is what gets them up in the morning.

Proof can be found among the highly successful entrepreneurs who launch a series of businesses. Even when they can well afford to retire and live the leisurely life many people fantasize about, these entrepreneurs would rather be working on the next big idea. John Robbins took an early retirement at age forty after selling his mortgage finance company, bought a yacht, and golfed five days a week, only to discover that he really wanted to be working. In the process, he established a powerful legacy of enterprises imbued with deep understanding of the mortgage business and a strong sense of integrity; as a titan, he also became a spokesperson for the industry.

Titans are a unique subset among entrepreneurs. This rare

status is not defined by the size of the company or the financial success of the founder. Rather, becoming a titan entails an ability to scale a business not only with a breadth of multiple locations or additional product lines but with a depth of talent. The business may start with the entrepreneur, but very quickly transitions to the team. This is particularly important in people-intensive services businesses, such as those profiled in this book.

At the beginning, however, an entrepreneur is a person with a concept and a plan. The entrepreneurial mind-set is often instilled early. The most successful of business builders can trace a direct line back to an early job; consider Bill Sanders, founder of LaSalle Partners, who as a youngster sold refreshments through a hole in the fence at the local country club golf course, and serial entrepreneur Sam Zell, who "imported" *Playboy* magazine from the city to the suburbs with a hefty markup—at the age of twelve. Entrepreneurs work hard and consider their early tough jobs to be a badge of honor. These early stories also show an "entrepreneurial eye" for finding opportunities that lead to the top. For Sanders, it is real estate services, a business he practically invented and translated into a global empire. For Zell, it is following macro trends to identify opportunities in multiple businesses, enabling him to operate at the thirty-thousand-foot level while delegating day-to-day operations.

Entrepreneurial people are also adept at finding opportunities, and with seizing those that find them. Sometimes, they are en route to doing something else; take, for example, Rick Federico, who planned to go to law school until he spent the summer working at the restaurant his father had just purchased, a move that launched a career that took him through the major chains to become chairman and CEO of P.F. Chang's China Bistro. Or Bill Jensen, who thought a $2.50 an hour job at a ski resort was a perfect way to get paid for skiing, then stayed on and now is CEO of Intrawest, one of the premier ski resort operations in the world. As titans, they connect with an early passion for the business.

Even those who take over a family business, as Stuart Miller did with home builder Lennar Corporation, can make their own mark by seeing things differently and taking the business in a new direction. For Miller, that means listening closely to customers and providing new features in meaningful and sustainable ways. Becoming a titan requires honoring the past while navigating toward a future of one's own definition.

Entrepreneurs are constantly learning, starting with their businesses and what makes a meaningful difference in improving the customer experience. Business builders rigorously study their operations. Titans take it to the "nth degree," with a continual focus on improvement. Bill Marriott learned this discipline from his father, who regularly visited every restaurant in the family's chain; when he was young, Marriott often tagged along. As the head of Marriott International, Marriott has been known for making surprise visits to hotel properties around the world, not only to check quality and consistency, but to hear from the front-line employees.

Titans recognize that with the right team in place an operation can grow exponentially. This is a difficult leap for many entrepreneurs, whose hands-on natures can be formidable impediments to delegating authority to others. It takes an introspective and confident entrepreneur to recognize his weaknesses (for many, the devil truly is in the details of execution) and to purposefully hire and promote those who are strong in those areas. Noel Watson, chairman of Jacobs Engineering, a global colossus in engineering, construction, and infrastructure projects, knows that gaining market share means having the best team. For him, recruiting and retaining talent is everything.

Most uniquely, titans are teachers. For Julia Stewart of Dine-Equity, whose parents were both teachers, the skill may be inborn, but somehow this busy and ambitious executive, who is now CEO of a leading casual dining chain, has found time to mentor and coach others. In fact, she believes it is a critical skill for scaling a business across locally operated units.

Developing a team is also part of value creation that not only grows a business, but also attracts investment capital. Robert Johnson, who created a media empire with Black Entertainment Television (BET), demonstrated value generation as a business builder and now deploys capital as an investor in a variety of enterprises.

Entrepreneurs who become titans are able to assemble the pieces in such a way that the whole is a unique and value-added creation far greater than the individual parts. They don't just look at how big a company is getting (with a top-line, revenue focus), but how well it's doing, which draws attention to such things as profit margin, per store sales, and, of course, bottom-line profitability. For Paul Diaz, CEO of Kindred Healthcare, which emerged from Chapter 11 bankruptcy and then became part of the Fortune 500, measurement gauges the health of the organization and the crucial differences made in the lives of patients in terms of healing and wellness.

The transition from entrepreneur to titan also depends largely upon the culture that is built; in a very real sense it sets an expectation for behaviors and interactions, whether among employees or with customers. To a person, the titans profiled in this book could define their cultures in tangible terms that, not surprisingly, evoked excellence, commitment, integrity, attention to detail, and recognition that success can never be taken for granted.

The final word on becoming a titan is legacy. The businesses they build are intended to outlast them. Obviously, they cannot control the future or dictate what will come to pass, but they can establish a culture that allows their firms to pursue opportunities, create value, and develop their teams.

Becoming an entrepreneur is not easy, and only a very small number become titans. But why not you? If you find within yourself the characteristics of a successful business builder, if you have the passion and the drive, a commitment to excellence, the ability to turn a concept into a reality, and the desire to build a winning team, then you already have a head start. Learn from the examples of those who have come before. Then find your niche and enjoy the adventure.

NOTES

Chapter 2

1. Executive Profile, "Run for the Border," *Cornell Real Estate Review*, 2007, Vol. 5.
2. Ibid.
3. Ibid.

Chapter 3

1. Dan Neil, "The 50 Worst Cars of All Time," Time.com, 2007, accessed September 6, 2012, http://www.time.com/time/spe cials/2007/article/0,28804,1658545_1657867_1657781,00 .html#ixzz1xhWPp8NN.

Chapter 5

1. Mickey Meece, "Saturday Interview; Can IHOP Do for Apple-bee's What It Did for Itself?" *New York Times*, August 11, 2007, accessed September 6, 2012, http://query.nytimes.com/gst/ fullpage.html?res=9400E3DD173BF932A2575BC0A9619 C8B63.
2. Ibid.

Chapter 6

1. Adam Bryant, "No Ranting and Raving Is Permitted," *New York Times*, November 12, 2011, http://www.nytimes.com/ 2011/11/13/business/robert-l-johnson-anger-has-no-place -in-business.html?pagewanted=all.

2. Bryant, "No Ranting and Raving Is Permitted."
3. "Black Entertainment Television," Museum of Broadcast Communications, accessed September 6, 2012, http://www.museum .tv/eotvsection.php?entrycode=blackenterta.

Chapter 7

1. "Setting an Example," *Leaders Magazine*, Vol. 35, No. 2, 2012, accessed August 8, 2012, http://www.leadersmag.com/issues/ 2012.2_Apr/PDFs/LEADERS-Sam-Zell-Equity-Group-Invest ments.pdf.
2. "History," Equity Group Investments, accessed August 8, 2012, http://egizell.com/history.html.
3. "Setting an Example," *Leaders Magazine*.

Chapter 8

1. "P.F. Chang's Federico Named 2012 Norman Award Winner," *Nation's Restaurant News*, April 30, 2012, http://nrn.com/arti cle/pf-chang%E2%80%99s-federico-named-2012-norman -award-winner-%E2%80%A9#ixzz234Ve9b3f.

Chapter 9

1. "CEO Awards, Most Respected CEOs," *CEO Q* magazine, 2010, http://www.ceoqmagazine.com/mostrespectedceos/ceo _kinderedhealthcare_pauldiaz.htm.

INDEX

A

accountability
  board of directors, 32
  bottom line and, 55–68
  CEO, 107–108
  empowerment and, 89–90
  integrity and, 142–143,
    144–145
  Marriott on, 12–13
  metrics and, 135
  rope theory and, 99–100
acquisitions and mergers,
    65–66
advisers
  boards of directors as, 30–32
  Marriott on, 14–15, 19
  Miller on, 44
  Sanders on, 30
  self-knowledge and, 67
affinity skills, 158–162
alignment
  of culture with strategy,
    28–30
  innovation and, 49–51
  rope theory on, 99–100

American Mortgage Network,
    140, 150–151
American Residential Investment
    Trust, 140, 149–150
American Residential Mortgage
    Corporation, 139, 140–141,
    149
Anderson, Stuart, 71
Anixter International Inc., 102
Applebee's, 70, 71, 81–82
Archstone, 34

B

balanced scorecard, 133–134
Batista, Fulgencio, 128
Bennigan's, 115
Big Bowl, 121
Black Angus Cattle Company
    Restaurants, 71
Black Entertainment Television,
    83–96
Blackstone Group, 102
boards of directors, 30–32,
    108

INDEX

Bob's Big Boy, 14
Boy Scouts of America,
    128–129
brand equity, 11
brand extension, 117–119
Brinker, Norman, 113, 115
Brinker International, 116, 120,
    121
Broadcasting & Cable magazine,
    91
Burger King, 70, 71
butterfly effect, 52
buy-in, 72–74, 88–90

C

candor, 31
Capital Trust, 102
Carl's Jr., 70, 71
Carlyle Group, 95
CarrAmerica Realty Corporation,
    34
Castro, Fidel, 128
CEOs
    chairman role and, 98–99
    dismissals, board involvement
        in, 31
    employee relationships with,
        129, 148–149
    performance evaluation for,
        107–108
    performance objectives for,
        15–16
    succession planning, 16,
        63–64

challenges
    addressing, 60
    boards of directors and,
        31–32
    integrity in facing, 46–48,
        139–153
    perseverance and, 17–18
    preparing for, 80–82
    Stewart on, 80–82
character, 2–3. *See also* discipline;
    integrity
Chase Manhattan Bank, 149
Chiang, Celia, 118
Chiang, Philip, 117–118
Chili's, 115–116
coaching and mentoring, 3,
    69–82, 172
    attracting, 117
    Jensen in, 166–167
    Marriott on, 18–19
    Miller on, 40–43
    Watson on, 63
collaboration, 106–107, 131
Colorado Ski Hall of Fame,
    160
commitment, 3, 89
common sense, 63
communication skills
    buy-in and, 73–74
    with customers, 150
    empowering others and,
        88–90
    honesty and, 76–78
    learning from others and,
        78–80

listening, 78–80
compensation, 2
  bottom line and, 62
  integrity and, 145
  Marriott on, 11–12
  rewarding effort and, 78
  strategic alignment and,
    28–30
confidence, 4
  in hiring, 19
  humility and, 86–87
  opportunities and, 110
  value creation and, 94–95
Connor, Mike, 114–115
Cornell Real Estate Review,
  29–30, 34
cost management, 135
Courtyard by Marriott, 15
Covanta Holding Corporation,
  102
Craig, Kyle, 70
culture, 2, 172–173
  bottom line and, 62
  employee match with,
    122–124
  empowered, 89–90
  innovation and, 50–51
  integrity and, 144–145, 151–153
  leadership and, 142–143
  Marriott on, 12–13
  owning mistakes and, 76–78
  Sanders on, 28–30, 37–38
  transparency and, 106–107
customer satisfaction, 3
  2 percent difference and, 157

bottom line and, 59–60
emotional connections and,
  90–93
employees in, 131
engagement and, 83–84
feedback and, 125–126
focus on, 129
Marriott on, 11
Miller on, 44
Robbins on, 146
strategic relevance and,
  29–30
understanding customer needs
  and, 13–14

D

Darden Restaurants, 119, 120
decision making, 92
  information for, 163, 165
  integrity and, 142
  problem solving and, 16–21
desire to serve, 165
detail, attention to, 157
development, employee, 3
  bottom line and, 62
  Federico on, 122–124
  Marriott on, 11–12
  value building and, 135–136
Diaz, Paul J., 125–137, 172
  on building value, 135–136
  influences on, 127–129
  on teams, 130–133
DineEquity, Inc., 69–82
discipline, 2–3, 127, 171

discipline (*continued*)
  bottom line and, 56, 62–66
  extra effort and, 157, 164
due diligence, 48, 80–81

E
Edsel, 49–50
education, 26. *See also* learning
efficiency improvement, 135
effort, 5, 155–167, 169
ego, 4
  fear and, 36
  learning from mistakes and,
   79–80
  Sanders on, 32–35
  team building and, 132
emotional maturity, 132
employees
  achieving vision with, 88–90
  attracting and retaining strong,
   63
  bottom line and, 60–62
  complementary skills in,
   45
  cultural fit with, 29–30
  customer orientated, 2
  developing, 3
  expectations on, 72–73
  hiring smart, 19
  Marriott on, 11–12
  mentoring, 69–82
  relationships with, 12–13, 129,
   148–149
  rope theory on, 99–100

  training, 11–12
empowerment, 89–90, 121
engagement, 6
  achieving vision through,
   88–90
  CEO influence on, 148
  failure to create, 121
  passion and, 163
  value creation and, 83–84
entrepreneurs
  born vs. made, 101, 164–165
  bottom line and, 55–68
  business incubators, 97–110
  desire of to control their own
   destiny, 149–152
  exit strategy for, 35–36
  expectations of others and,
   71–72, 160–161
  in family businesses, 40–46
  impatience in, 69
  as investors, 95–96
  maturation of business and,
   58
  metrics and, 55–68, 126
  opportunities seen by, 24
  self-knowledge and, 51–52
  serial, 36, 48
  success rate of, 1
  titans vs., 155, 169–173
Equity Group Investments,
  97–110
Equity Lifestyle Properties, Inc.,
  102
Equity Office Properties Trust,
  102

INDEX

evaluation process, 107–108
execution, 2–3, 88–90, 107, 149
exit strategy, 35–36
expansion, 117–119
expectations
  career paths and, 71–72,
    160–161
  mortgage industry, 140–141
  Stewart on, 72–74

F
failure
  engagement and, 121
  fear of, innovation and, 50
  learning from, 50–51, 65–66,
    163
  learning from others', 78–80
  owning, 76–78
  risk management and, 92, 93
  taking yourself too seriously
    and, 108–110
  Watson on, 65–66
Fairfield Inn & Suites, 15
Farrell's Ice Cream Parlors, 14
fear, 36, 50, 86–87
Federico, Richard "Rick," 111–
    124, 170–171
  career path of, 114–117
  on employee development,
    122–124
  expansion by, 117–119
  influences on, 111–114
  on power of ownership,
    120–121

feedback, 108, 125–126, 132
  metrics and, 134–135
Fibreboard Resort Group, 160
finances
  acquisitions/mergers and,
    65–66
  focus on the bottom line,
    55–68
  globalization and, 65–66
  integrity and, 142
  Marriott on, 14, 19–21
  Miller on, 43–44
  patience with, 37
  synergies in, 65
  value creation and, 94–95
financial crisis of 2008, 20–21, 51
  General Motors in, 59
  Robbins in, 140–153
Fleming, Paul, 117–118
focus, 117
Ford Motor Company, 49–50
franchises, 74–75, 77–78,
    120–121
fun, having at work, 3, 5–22

G
GE Capital, 24, 35–36
General Motors, 59
globalization, 65–66, 105
goals
  CEO, 16
  monitoring, 133, 134
  value building and, 135–136
Grady's Goodtimes, 113–114

H

Hewlett-Packard, 157
hiring
  bottom line and, 60–62
  for collaboration, 131
  cultural fit and, 29–30
  for cultural match, 122–124
  global attitude in, 61
  humility and, 86–87
  leadership in, 48
  Marriott on, 19
Holiday Inn, 13
home of the future, 50–51
Homex Development, 104
honesty, 76–78
Host Airport, 14
Host Hotels and Resorts,
  6, 20
Hot Shoppes, 7, 10, 12–13
humility, 86–87, 114

I

identity, professional, 158–162
incentives, 2, 11–12. *See also*
  compensation
incubators, entrepreneurs as,
  97–110
information. *See also* learning
  for decision making, 163, 165
  Marriott on sources for, 14–15,
  19
innovation, 39
  collaborative culture and,
  106–107

listening and, 79–80
Marriott on, 14
in mature markets, 40
Miller on, 47–51
through improvement, 58–59
integration, 2
integrity, 3, 16, 139–153
  influence of, 143–145
  Miller on, 40, 46–48
International Development Corp,
  26
International House of Pancakes,
  70–71, 72–74, 77–78
Intrawest, 155, 162, 171
introspection, 51–52
investors, 95–96, 172

J

Jacobs, Joseph J., 56, 63
Jacobs Engineering Group Inc.,
  55–68
Jensen, William A. "Bill,"
  155–167
  career path of, 158–162, 171
  on evaluating opportunities,
  160–162
  influences on, 156–157
  as mentor, 166–167
  on outworking competitors,
  162–164
Jobs, Steve, 58
Johnson, Robert L., 83–96,
  172
  career path of, 85–88

on emotional connections,
90–93
investment ventures of, 95–96
on value creation, 94–95
on vision and employees,
88–90
Jones Lang LaSalle, 24, 33
Jones Lang Wootton, 33

K
Karcher, Carl, 70, 71
Kindred Healthcare, Inc.,
125–137

L
La Quinta, 14
LaSalle Partners Ltd., 23–37
leadership, 16
accountability and, 142–143
control in, 44
generational differences in,
41–46
integrity in crises, 139–153
mentoring and, 74–76
owning mistakes and, 76–78
Robbins on, 147–148
rope theory and, 99–100
styles of and business
situations, 48, 66–67
vision and, 89–90
Leaders Magazine, 101
learning, 171. *See also* coaching
and mentoring

about the business/industry, 3,
23–38, 41–42
to broaden skill sets, 127
communication skills and,
88–90
lifelong, 42
from mentoring, 75–76
Miller on, 41–42
from mistakes, 50–51,
65–66, 163
from mistakes and successes of
others, 78–80, 119
from teams, 132
legacy, 52, 136, 173
integrity and, 139–153
mentoring and, 166–167
Lennar Corporation, 39–53,
171
loan securitization, 148
loyalty, 11
loyalty programs, 13–14
luck, 92, 117, 159
Lurie, Robert, 101, 102–103

M
Macaroni Grill, 116
Mammoth Mountain, 159–160
management by wandering
around, 129
Mandarin Restaurant, 118
Marriott, J. W. Bill, Jr., 5–21,
129
discipline of, 171
father's influence on, 9–15

Marriott, J. W. Bill, Jr. (*continued*)
  love of work, 7–9
  on problem solving, 16–21
Marriott, J. Willard, 6–7, 9–15
Marriott, Richard, 6
Marriott Rewards, 13–14
Marriott Twin Bridges Hotel, 9
Martin, John, 70
mature businesses, 58
McCoy, Dave, 159–160, 166
McKinsey & Company, 29
McLarty, Mack, 95
measurement and metrics, 55–
  68, 125–137, 172
  of CEO performance, 107–108
  employee development and,
  62
  Stewart on, 72–73
menial labor, 86–87
Miller, Leonard, 40–46, 52
Miller, Stuart, 39–53, 171
  on innovation, 48–51
  on integrity, 46–48
  on leadership differences,
  43–46
  on managing father-son
  dynamic, 40–43
  self-knowledge of, 51–52
Modern Healthcare magazine,
  127
Mortgage Bankers Association,
  139, 140–141, 151
Mortgage Banking Magazine, 151
motivation, 5–6, 136
  CEO influence on, 148

ownership and, 120–121
  self-, 87, 88
Museum of Broadcast
  Communication, 84–85, 91

N
National Basketball Association,
  84
National Cable Television
  Association, 91–92
National Football League, 88
Nation's Restaurant News,
  112, 113
niches, finding underserved, 3,
  23–25, 39–53
Norman Award, 112, 113

O
Olive Garden, 119
opportunity, 24, 88, 170–171
  economic conditions and,
  152
  fear and, 36
  game-changing, 164
  industry boundaries and,
  104–105
  outcomes-based thinking on,
  160–162
  perspective in finding,
  104–105
  watching for, 49
  Zell on recognizing, 100–105
optimism, 112

Orville Bean's Flying Machine
   and Fix-It Shops, 115
Outback Steakhouse, 120
outcomes-based thinking, 160–162
owner's approach, 98
ownership, emotional connection
   of, 120–121

P

partners, 120–121
passion, 3, 5–6, 127, 149
   effort and, 162
   engagement and, 163
   Marriott on, 7–9
patience, 37, 49, 69
Pei Wei Asian Diner, 113, 119
people skills, 107
performance
   bottom line and, 55–68
   expectations on, 72–73
   feedback on, 108
   goals for, 16
   synergies in, 65
perseverance, 17–18, 26
personality, 112
personalization, 150
perspective
   balancing big picture and idea
      generation, 99
   balancing long-term and short-
      term, 59–60
   big picture, 98
   on generational differences, 45
   macro vs. micro, 104–105

Sanders on, 32–35
Peters, Tom, 129
P.F. Chang's China Bistro, Inc.,
   111–124
PharMerica Corporation, 126
pilot errors, 92, 93
problem solving, 16–21, 60, 110
procrastination, 60
Prologis, 35–36

R

real estate investment trusts
   American Residential
      Investment Trust, 140,
      149–150
   Equity Group, 102
   LaSalle Partners, 24–37
   Marriott, 6
Regas, Bill, 113–114
Regency Centers, 34
relevance, 27–28, 45
Renaissance, 15
respect, 100
retirement, 169
Rickenbacker, Eddie, 10
right-sizing, 118–119
risk
   calculated, 111–124
   delegating, 99–100
   in expansion/brand extensions,
      117–119
   identifying and managing, 92,
      93
   integrity and, 142

Ritz-Carlton, 15
Robbins, John, 139–153, 169
  desire of to control his destiny,
    149–152
  influences on, 145–148
  on the shadow of integrity,
    143–145
Robert H. Lurie Comprehensive
  Cancer Center, 102
role models
  fathers as, 18–19, 40–43,
    111–112
  Federico, 111–114
  Jensen, 159–160
  Marriott, 9–15
  Miller, 40–43
Romano, Phil, 116
Romano's Macaroni Grill,
  116
rope theory, 99–100

S
Samuel Zell and Robert Lurie
  Real Estate Center, 102–103
Samuel Zell & Robert H. Lurie
  Institute for Entrepreneurial
  Studies, 102–103
Sanders, William "Bill," 23–37
  on culture, 28–30
  early life of, 24–27, 170
  on strategy relevance, 27–28
Security Capital Group, 24,
  34–35, 35–36
self-knowledge, 51–52, 67, 104

serendipity, 117, 159
shareholder relations, 16
Shaw, Bill, 19–20
single-mindedness, 117
SpringHill Suites, 15
stakeholder relations, 16
Steak and Ale Restaurants,
  114–115
Stewart, Julia, 69–82, 172
  on buy-in, 72–74
  on career paths, 71–72
  on challenges, 80–82
  on learning from others'
    mistakes, 78–80
  on owning mistakes, 76–78
  on success through others,
    74–75
Strategic Growth Bank
  Incorporated, 36
strategy
  buy-in on, 72–74
  generational differences and,
    41
  innovation and, 49–51
  relevance of, 27–28, 45
subprime mortgages, 140–153
success
  effort in, 162–164
  employees in, 61–62
  infallibility vs., 108–110
  perspective on, 32–35
  rate of entrepreneurial, 1
  rewarding others in, 100
  through others, 74–75
succession

legacy and values in, 136
mentoring for, 76
planning, 16, 63–64
sustainability
    integrity and, 144–145
    relevant strategy and, 27–28
    teams in, 60–62
    Watson on, 59–60

T
Taco Bell, 70, 71
teams, 3, 171–172
    bottom line and, 60–62
    championing, 132–133
    leading, 130–131, 142–143
    metrics for, 134–135
    Sanders on, 29–30
    success based on, 130–133
    value building and, 135–136
timing, 92, 105
titans
    career paths of, 98
    entrepreneurs vs., 155,
        169–173
    legacy of, 167
    team building by, 131
training, 11–12
transparency, 106–107
    around metrics, 135
    integrity and, 144
Tribune Company, 109
trust, 31, 144
turf-protecting mentality, 106–107
2 percent difference, 3, 155–167

U
U.S. Army Intelligence,
    146

V
Vail Resorts Management
    Company, 161–162
value creation, 83–96,
    172
    measuring, 133–135
values, 52. *See also* culture;
    integrity
Viacom, 85
Video Soul program, 91
vision, 2–3, 15–16, 67
    buy-in on, 72–74
    communicating, 88–90
    emotional connections and,
        90–93
    engagement with, 83–85,
        88–90
    value creation from,
        83–96
voice-activated technology,
    50–51

W
Wachovia, 151
walking in the back door,
    47
Watson, Noel, 55–68
    on acquisitions/mergers,
        65–66

INDEX

Watson, Noel (*continued*)
    career path of, 55–57
    on discipline, 62–66
    on leadership, 66–67
    on teams, 60–62
  work ethic, 3, 86
    2 percent difference and,
      155–167
    Marriott on, 8
    Watson on, 64

Z

Zell, Sam, 97–110
    career path of, 104–105, 169
    on culture, 106–107
    opportunity recognition by,
      100–105
    rope theory of, 99–100
    on taking yourself too
      seriously, 108–110